"*Finding Daddy* is a real life "fictional drama" that will make you laugh, cry, and relate..."

Aaron Bebo, author of *Change For A Dollar*

"New author Renita Gibbs has crafted an engaging, yet poignant story in her debut novel about a young girl looking for love from the first man in her life, her daddy. Definitely a recommended read!"

Michelle Larks, author of *Faith*

"Praise for Renita Gibbs' first novel, *Finding Daddy*. This true-to-life story beautifully details the pain and disillusionment that growing up without a father in the home can bring to a person's life, particularly that of a young and impressionable girl. This timely piece further brings home the seriousness of family connectivity and how this cohesiveness, or lack of it, ultimately affects our children."

Nikki D. Bosompem of Insight Editing Services, LLC

# *ACKNOWLEDGEMENTS*

First I would like to thank God for giving me the strength to complete the assignment from Him.

The writing of this book has been a wonderfully transformative yet sometimes difficult experience for me. I could not have completed this book without the help and support of a number of important people in my life who contributed in countless ways to my experience in writing the book.

My gratitude is to my family who generously shared me with this manuscript. To my husband Derick Sr. my life partner of almost 14 years. Derick you have been my guiding force in helping me muster the courage to step out and find my way. You are truly the breath beneath my wings.

Thanks to my boys Derick Jr. and Daniel for believing in and encouraging their mother. Thanks for the necessary time to think, write, and rewrite. Both Derick Jr. and Daniel were at my side each day that I worked on this book. Thanks for giving mommy the quiet time I needed to keep me focused on what truly matters.

Thanks Aaron Bebo, my writing partner. He is a gifted writer with the ability to step into the story and bring things to life. Your talent and expertise have been invaluable. Thank you for assisting me in producing the best book possible. I feel so blessed to have you in my corner. Thanks for encouraging me to share the story in my own voice. Thank you for the guidance and being so generous without limited time and your writing talent to bring this project to completion.

Thanks to Stacey Randle, my partner, for your continuing support in everything I undertake in this life. You are invariably in my corner personally and spiritually. Thank you for making the renewal of my vows possible. You put in so many long hours and stayed up preparing for that event. You are MY PERSONAL

CATERING GIRL. YOU DID IT AGAIN. THE FOOD WAS DELICIOUS. THANKS FOR ALL THE LONG HOURS OF COOKING.

Thanks Shawonda Gates for introducing me to my writing partner and thanks for being understanding. I appreciate you for allowing your house to be open every time I needed to talk or sit down with my writing partner. Thanks for just being real folks. We did it!!!!

Thanks to my airline crew for all the encouraging words. I really appreciated all the love and support. Thank you for reading my first chapter and offering priceless comments and feed back to help fine tune the book.

Thanks to all my guests. Each and every one of you have brought a special element in my life because you were there. Thank you for the heartfelt moments, the laughter, the tears, the joy, and encouragement.

Thanks to my mother, Mary Wilson, for being the lady you are. Thanks for instilling strength in me. You demonstrated how to be a strong and powerful woman through your humility, grace, and service. Thanks for being supportive and for all the unconditional love. I love you, mother.

Thanks to my daddy; I only had you for about 6 months, but thanks for the time we spent together. I finally have closure with my daddy-daughter relationship. I miss you everyday, daddy. But hey, I know you are up in heaven having a ball. Until we meet again…love, your baby girl.

Thanks to my brother Benedict Bennett. I love you so much! Thanks for standing in the gap and taking care of me when I was younger. Thanks for all the fun and sad memories. Thanks for walking on this journey with me.

Thanks to my sister Robernett Nesbitt. I love you so much. Thanks for walking on this journey with me.

Thanks to Apostle Sandra Appleberry, my spiritual mother. You have shown me how to love when its hurts, taught me how to forgive repeatedly and always keep the faith. You have been an example of strength and perseverance. Thanks for making my vow renewal a special day in my life. I will always love you.

Thanks to my graphic designer, Leonard Eskridge, for your countless hours developing the cover. You are much appreciated.

Special thanks to Ms. Lucy McNeil. Thanks for taking care of my daddy and being there with him through the good and bad times. Even though daddy is gone, I will always be there for you.

Thanks to my daddy's brother Clarence Pope. Thanks so much for being who you are. I'm so glad you and Ms. Freddie are a part of my life.

Special thanks to my girls, Vonita Eason-Marion, Anna Wester, Kathy Walters, and Teresa Smith for allowing me to go home and get some rest while you ladies worked together and made sure things were back in order at the building...

# *FOREWORD*

This book is dedicated to the many fatherless children in the world who travel on cobblestones in search of a connection that was lost somewhere in their lives. A connection to a figure they expected during the nurturing process, supplying guidance and applying love with understanding. More importantly, the role of the father being present is to instill self worth and a sense of affiliation to something that is of themselves.

We see it all too often, a woman being forced into the role of a man once the correlation, rapport, bond, liaison, or link between a couple ends on bad terms and there is a child involved. There is also the huge number of incarcerated males which also plays a major role in this broken connection, among other things like infidelity and plain old irresponsibility. Sometimes these behaviors are inherited flaws from a cycle that has been repeated throughout time.

Has the term "father" or "daddy" lost the fiber of its meaning? Should the search for that missing connection be abandoned? I think not. I offer this work of fiction as a voice and possibly a map for the many who are still on a quest for that connection. I pen these characters in a knowing voice for all those who are on a journey to finding daddy.

~Renita Wilson-Gibbs

Throughout my career of teaching, I've taught many children without a father in the home. Not all of them show the effectives of their environment because there are those who have excelled while reaching out for the stars. But there are those children who tend to seek a place of belonging through their world of day dreaming. They are those smart, talented kids who spend most of their time in class wondering why, but can't seem to understand. They sometimes display a sense of loneliness and low self-esteem, while struggling to give their best in their limited work and class participation. They act out while striving for excellence and they seek love while showing no fear of discipline. These are the kids who need someone to talk to. That's where I believe we as educators come in. Putting on one of our many hats called "care" and helping these children seek out their greatest potentials that lie beneath that quiet storm. Finding Daddy is definitely a must read!

~Carolyn Anderson West, Educator

All children are born into this world innocent. As they grow up, they are profoundly influenced by their families, friends, teachers, communities, as well as by TV, movies, music and the internet. As a social service/mental health provider, I have seen children affected by their home environment the most and this can cause an increasing negative effect over time. Including, but not limited to juvenile delinquency, teen pregnancy, violence and even incarceration.

I believe that this work that Renita has put into print is extremely powerful and effective. Not necessarily because of the information, which I am sure will positively contribute to the personal development of the women and young girls who will read it, but primarily because it's an outflow of her life experience.

I commend my dear friend Renita for her sensitivity and for her appreciation of the gift that God has placed in her to share with young girls and women around the world who wish to "Find Their Daddy". Finding daddy is crucial to every little girl.

~M. Simpson
Director of Social Work, South Carolina

## *DEDICATION*

I dedicate this book to my spiritual friend Dr. Eunice Strange and Judy Talley. I feel so honored and thankful to have been blessed with such caring friends. Dr. Eunice Strange will always have a special place in my heart for taking me to my daddy's house and going by to check on him when I could not get there. I also want to dedicate this book to you for making this possible. Ms. Judy Talley, I want to say thanks so much for introducing me too Dr. Eunice. Both of you ladies have a special place in my heart. Thank you for being God's example of unconditional love and his expression of unwavering faith. You two taught me how to stand and to love.

# CHAPTER 1
## MEETING DADDY FOR THE FIRST TIME

My sister and I hadn't slept a wink. It was 5:45 in the A.M. We could hear the early morning sounds outside our window as the neighborhood became alive with the sounds of the early morning laborers hustling off to their respective trades or professions. LaWanda, my sister, and I listened for the squeaky sound of Mama's brakes, even though we knew Mama wouldn't be home 'til round seven. She worked the grave yard shift from 11 to 7. LaWanda and I stayed home alone at night, but Mama made sure we had our dinner and had completed our chores and homework before she left for her shift. Often times, LaWanda and I were dead tired when we hit the sheets. Mama said she was raising women, not girls! She said we had to be strong and independent! That meant we were constantly being lectured and made to perform tasks in which mama considered our introduction into womanhood. Mama was strong and proud and didn't tolerate weakness from any of her kids, including Henry, my older brother. For a second I thought I heard the brakes on Mama's Grenada, but it was the cab that came and picked up Ms. Harris every morning. LaWanda and I talked and giggled beneath the covers all night. Right before Mama went to work last night, she told us to be up and ready to go when she got in from work in the morning. Mama told us that today we would be going to see our daddy. I was so excited. Mama barely spoke about our daddy much except to tell us how he was a ...well, I can't repeat after Mama. We went into Mama's room and got the old photo album she kept in the third drawer of the chest with her other important papers. We looked at the images of ourselves being held by our daddy. He was so handsome. LaWanda swore she had his smile. We must have run to the mirror two dozen times flashing our pearly whites trying to mimic the smile on the face in the image. We wondered if he looked the same. Would he remember us? We were so small the last time he saw us. It didn't matter; today we were finally going to meet Daddy.

    I wished our older brother, Henry, was home. He had been hauled off by the law two weeks ago. People had come and told Mama that Henry had been breaking into houses. I didn't believe that! Henry didn't have to steal, Mama gave us everything. We were some of the best dressed kids in the projects. Yeah, I said the projects! Besides, why would Henry be out stealing when he knew everybody knew Mama and she would kill him. Someone was always coming to tell Mama *something*. Henry was old enough to remember daddy. I didn't remember those days in the photos when he cradled me and my sister in his arms and smiled at Mama. My brother Henry told us stories about the man I only knew as daddy. He told us lots of stories. He told us how our daddy wasn't his daddy and how he was a very big reason why our daddy had left. We would sit and listen to Henry for hours and then we would all be crying and hugging. I loved my brother, but a part of me had a love for the man Mama called "no good" and who my brother hated…the man who had left us; the man that I only knew as daddy.

    I had just finished dressing when Mama came through the door. "Is ya'll ready?" Mama asked as she walked right past our room heading toward her bedroom. "Who's been in my drawers?" I heard Mama ask from her bedroom.

    LaWanda and I looked at each other. We had forgotten to put the photo album back. LaWanda spoke up. "I did Mama. I got the old photo album with the pictures of daddy."

    Silence. We stood in our room just staring at each other scared to move. We heard Mama come out of her room, then we heard the bathroom door close and the shower water start running. We both let out a sigh of relief for the moment. LaWanda rushed to get the photo album from her bed. We stole one last glance at the photo of daddy before she crept back into Mama's room to return it to the drawer. When Mama emerged from the bathroom she was sharp in a Liz Baker navy blue pants suit with matching navy blue Rockport Barbella Pumps. She only brought those pumps out on Easter. She must really be trying to look good for daddy; she had

# Finding Daddy

even put the hot comb on the eye of the stove and took it to her hair. Mama gave us the once over, grabbed her purse and ushered us out the door. We got into Mama's silver Grenada and she started the car. Before she pulled out, she turned to me and said, "Lucinda, when we get to this courthouse, I don't want you to say a word 'less I tell you to speak. You understand me?"

"Yes ma'am," we said in unison. My heart sank. Why were we going to the courthouse? We were supposed to be going to see our daddy! Before I could stop myself, I uttered, "Mama, why we going to the courthouse? We s'pose to be going to see daddy." I think LaWanda flinched causing me to do so as well. You didn't question Mama. You just went along, but I had just crossed that line. I was so excited about going to see daddy, I wasn't thinking.

"You just sit there and be quiet 'less I tell you to speak! You understand?!"

"Yes ma'am." I sat back in the seat disappointed. I just kept thinking about the man in the photo album, the four of us together. Mama looked so happy. I had never seen Mama look so happy. I was so confused and all I knew was I wanted to see my daddy.

We rode downtown with the windows down. The early morning sun was already beaming brightly. The man on the car's radio said it would reach ninety-five degrees today and it was only the third day of summer. Normally, LaWanda and I would be at our grandmother's house helping her out because she was legally blind. We would go to her house and clean. I use to love to sweep the porch so I could listen to Nana talk about God and hum church hymns as she rocked back in forth in her rocker. She told us stories about our dad, too. She said daddy was a strong man, fine mannered and well liked. A big flirt with the women, whatever that meant. Nana said he was the worst kind of man and was no good for Mama. I didn't care though. Today I wanted to see that man, my daddy. Mama pulled into the courthouse parking lot. We all got out of the car and checked ourselves for wrinkles or loose hairs. The sun glared off the burgundy top of the Grenada. Satisfied, Mama began moving toward the courthouse steps. Just before we reached the steps Mama turned to us and said, "Your daddy should be here already."

My heart skipped a beat. Did she say daddy was here? As we entered the courthouse, the butterflies in my stomach felt like they were breaking out of their cocoons. I felt my heartbeat against my eardrum. I'm sure my smile lit up the entire building. I searched among the sea of faces we passed as we walked, looking for a match to the image in the photo album. Mama's heels clicked against the marble floor creating a symphony along with the sound of our hard bottoms as we stepped alongside her. We tried to keep up with her purposeful stride. We entered the courtroom and I immediately scanned the pews for the image in the picture again. Mama knelt down close to me and my sister and pointed, "That's your daddy right there." The man she pointed at briefly looked in our direction and then turned his head back toward the front of the courtroom where the judge, a salt and pepper haired white man with a huge, sagging jawline and cold eyes was scolding a man for failure to support his children. A homely looking woman stood next to the man holding a boy around my age that looked just like the man the judge was speaking to. Mama ushered us into a row directly across from my daddy. I stared at him, seeing the outline of my features in his face. He looked over at us, his face devoid of expression. I noticed how immaculately dressed he was; his hair was cut neat and short and his clothes were pressed and fit him well. I caught him looking over at us again and smiled, he quickly turned his head with no acknowledgment. It didn't matter. By this time I had realized that the meeting I thought was going to take place between my daddy and I was actually a meeting between Mama, the old white man, and my daddy. I also realized another thing: My daddy didn't want to be there. Neither did I. Mama should've just invited him to the house. I wanted him to look over at me again so I could see his face. Just when I thought he was going to turn to look at us again, the clerk called Mama's name.

  Mama directed my sister and I to the front of the courtroom to stand before the judge. My daddy stood opposite us with his head held high and his shoulders squared as he stood before the white man with the long black dress. The judge looked at all our faces as he shuffled through some papers before him. When he spoke, he looked directly at my daddy. "Mr. Wilson you have been petitioned to this court by a Helen Wilson, seeking child support for LaWandaWilson and Lucinda Wilson. The petition before the court shows you live in North Carolina. You are currently a Staff Sergeant in the U.S. Military." The judge paused and looked up

# Finding Daddy

from the papers he was reading with a questioning look.

"Yes sir."

My daddy's voice was so sure and confidant. I felt those butterflies in my stomach again. The judge continued, "Mr. Wilson I know the military allocates funds to a...," the judge cleared his throat, "a Staff Sergeant. Is there a reason the court is not aware of that would explain why these funds are not being allotted to Ms. Wilson for the care of your children?"

"Yes sir, your Honor. The children in question...," my daddy paused and looked over at my sister and me, then he looked at my mother, "are not mine, your Honor. I request a paternity test."

I didn't understand what it was my daddy said, but it sent my mother into a rage. "Dammit Billy! You know damn well these ya' damn kids. You dirty low down…"

Mama was cut off by the judge banging a wooden hammer on his desk. The judge pointed the wooden hammer at my mother. "Ms. Wilson! You will control yourself in my courtroom or you will be removed." The judge turned to my daddy, still pointing the wooden hammer. "Mr. Wilson, are you sure you want the court to order paternity in this matter because I forewarn you, if you are determined to be the biological father of these children, you will be very sorry for wasting the court's time." The judge lowered the wooden hammer, picked up a pen, and began scribbling on some papers. "The court orders paternity determination in the above mentioned matter. Mr. Wilson, you will submit a specimen for analysis. Ms. Wilson, you will be responsible for the children in the matter of submitting blood to determine paternity in this case. The court orders that these specimens be provided no later than five business days from the date of the court's ruling on this order. This case will be put back on the calendar for July 5, 1977 at which time I will make a ruling for support, past and present, if the test determines a just and true claim has been brought before this court by the plaintiff, Ms. Wilson. Next case on the calendar."

Just like that, the butterflies that had been gathering in my stomach all morning turned to knots. I didn't know what paternity meant, but I knew my daddy didn't want us. Mama cursed all the way home, using that word "paternity" in between her outbursts of obscenities.

# *CHAPTER 2*
## *CHILLIN' IN THE NEIGHBORHOOD*

Aunt Shirley lived on the east side of Augusta. I loved going to her house. We all gathered there on Sundays after church where she would cook for everyone. Aunt Shirley lived in a big peach colonial home. On hot days like today we would all be in the backyard under the patio with the perfect Eucalyptus umbrella lounge tables set upon the colorful, stone patio surface. LaWanda and I would run around the huge manicured lawn in the backyard, careful not to collect any dirt or grass stains on our Sunday dresses. Aunt Shirley always seemed to be there for all of us. Nana would pull LaWanda and I to the side and quiz us on what we had been learning in school. Everything would be great, especially when Henry was with us. I missed my brother so much. Mama said he should be home in a couple of months. It already seemed like he had been gone for so long. Mama had taken us to see him a few times since he had been gone. He always smiled so bright when he saw us. I couldn't wait until he was back home.

Mama pulled into Aunt Shirley's driveway behind Uncle Harvey's Mercedes Benz. He was leaning against the car smiling.

He gave Mama a big hug as she walked up the driveway. "Hey sis. How you been?"

Mama smiled and sighed, "I'm fine. Just waiting to get back into court and make Robert take care of his responsibility. I just can't believe he looked right at them in that courtroom and denied them flat out without blinking an eye! How could he do that?"

"I know, sis. But God is good, and he watches out for all his angels," Uncle Harvey said, reaching down to take me in his arms. "How has my angel been?" he asked, smiling at me.

"Fine," I said.

He placed a kiss on my cheek and put me down. Next he

lifted LaWanda into his arms. "How's my baby? You eatin' good. I see you getting heavy," Uncle Harvey laughed as he playfully poked a finger in LaWanda's stomach. She giggled and squirmed in his arms. He put her down after giving her a peck on the cheek. He reached his hand inside his pantsuit pocket and pulled out his bankroll. Uncle Harvey always had a big bankroll. He found a couple of dollars and gave LaWanda and me a dollar each.

We thanked him and asked where Aunt Beverly was. "She inside seasoning up some pork chops for Nana." Aunt Beverly was Uncle Harvey's wife. She was our favorite aunt after Aunt Shirley.

"Ya'll go on in the house and speak to your Nana and aunties," Mama said. As we headed inside, I heard Mama say to Uncle Harvey, "I can't wait until I see Bobby's face in court Tuesday when the judge reads those paternity results."

I hope Mama didn't start talking about our daddy today with Nana and the others. She would always start ranting and crying, calling me and my sister, putting us on display until everyone agreed with her that Robert was our father. I was still too young to fully understand paternity. I just thought our daddy didn't want us. Mama said he had moved away to take care of some other woman and her child. But the court was going to make him take care of us. I wondered if the court would make him come back to live with us and leave that other woman. I wondered if he held the other woman's child the way he held us in the photo.

Aunt Shirley gave LaWanda and I candy apples and let us sit in her bedroom to watch T.V. We loved hanging out in Aunt Shirley's room when we came over. The room was lit with a red light bulb and had those cool felt pictures depicting men and women with Afros. The women in the pictures were usually topless with grass skirts, the men shirtless with some type of large cat's fur covering their privates. She had long wooden beads that hung from floor to ceiling on the outer perimeter of her water bed. There was a large cosmetic stand in the corner with all types of exotic body soaps and oils. Her dresser was full of bottled fragrances and body powders. The walls of the room were lined with racks full of shoes, and the room's walk-in closet was like a small department store. There were all types of dresses, blouses, and hats. She would allow us to play dress up sometimes and give us a squirt of perfume. I liked playing dress up, but what I really liked to do was climb the

## Finding Daddy

huge pecan tree in the front yard. LaWanda and I would climb the tree and gather as many pecans as we could in an old Easter basket.

We'd often get so carried away gathering pecans, we'd soil our dresses and dirty our shoes. Mama would have a fit. We may be grounded to the house for days after that. Depending on if Mama started drinking gin, we'd sometimes get a chance to change clothes once we got home before she noticed.

After we finished our candy apples, we decided to go play out front. We knew the joyful spirit that had touched my aunts and uncles earlier in church was now replaced with spirits bought in a bottle from the local package store. The gospel had stopped playing and the soul music had started. We went out to the backyard to ask Mama if we could go out front and play. LaWanda and I stepped out onto the patio and my other uncle, Clyde, was dancing with Nana, holding a plastic cup of "juice." Aunt Beverly was putting more meat on the grill, shaking her hips to the music as she did so. Mama spotted LaWanda and I and called us over to where she was sitting with Uncle Harvey, Clarence, and Aunt Shirley, beneath one of the umbrella tables. I knew Mama had been drinking; she was speaking very loudly and her eyes were bloodshot. "Look at my babies, ya'll," Mama said as we approached. "Look at these beautiful girls! How could anyone deny them? Low down dog of a man! I hope him and that tramp he's married to…"

"Hey, hey now sis, not in front of the girls. You gotta keep it cool. God will handle it. Don't go working yourself up, just be patient. You go back to court in a couple of days and it will be over."

"It ain't never going to be over! He ain't going to have no good luck. The way he treated me, Henry, and the girls!" Mama screamed, standing up on unsteady legs. She made her way to the table with the food on it and began making a plate.

Uncle Clarence pulled me and my sister close in an embrace and kissed us. "You girls go on out front and play. Don't go too far, okay?"

"Yes sir," we said.

Every time people started talking about our daddy they would send us to another room or outside to play. I didn't understand why no one wanted us to know about our daddy. Everyone always seemed to be angry with my daddy. I didn't understand it. I couldn't wait until we went back to court in a few days so I could see him again. Even though he said he wasn't our daddy in court last time, I knew that was my daddy. I just wanted him to hold me again like he did in the picture. I wanted to see him smile again. I wanted to laugh and play with my daddy like other little girls. I knew I always had a father in God, but I wanted my daddy.

As LaWanda and I stepped out into the hot sun, we saw Andrea and Angela. They were the twin girls from next door we sometimes played with when we came to Aunt Shirley's. The twins always seemed to have an adventure for us. Last time we were over here, the twins let us ride their bikes. We rode all over the neighborhood; we even went to Gurly's Market. Gurly's Market was on the other side of the railroad tracks. If Mama knew we had gone on the other side of the tracks, our bottoms would've gotten roasted. We made our way down the driveway toward the twins. "Why ya'll always come over here in those dresses? Ain't ya'll got no play clothes?"

I didn't like Angela much. She always seemed to be trying to boss LaWanda and me around because she was older. The twins were thirteen and had an older teenage sister named Thelma. Last time we went to their house, we saw Thelma kissing a boy. Yuck! Aunt Shirley said Thelma was going to be fast just like her Mama.

"These our church clothes. Our play clothes is at home," LaWanda said.

"Ya'll wanna go riding?" Andrea asked.

"Yes," I blurted out. I was hoping they would let us ride the bikes again. Even though LaWanda never let me ride her, it was still fun with her riding me. My bicycle at home was a lot smaller than the bike the twins let us share. I liked the big bike and so did LaWanda. As we went into their yard to get the bikes from the porch, Angela announced she would be riding Thelma's bike. Thelma's bike was the biggest. It was the kind with gears and it didn't have a banana seat. We had to help her get the bike off the porch, it was so big. We rode to Pennington King Park. I liked the park, it had all the swings and the seesaw worked. The kids in the projects we lived in broke the swings and seesaw so much that the people stopped fixing them. Now, the older kids hung out in the park smoking cigarettes and gambling. Henry used to hang out in

## Finding Daddy

the park sometimes, too, but he always kept an eye on us whenever we were outside. He was our protector.

We kept watch on the bicycles as we played on the swings and the merry-go-round. After awhile, Angela and Andrea said they wanted to go to the store. I remembered the dollar Uncle Harvey had given us earlier and I suddenly had the urge for a cold pop. We got back on the bicycles and headed toward the railroad tracks. Angela was leading the pack on the big bike. We could barely keep up. Once we crossed the railroad tracks, Angela slowed down, allowing us to catch up. I held on tight to LaWanda keeping watch for any dogs. Aunt Shirley had warned us long ago that the people on the other side of the tracks didn't like us coming over there. They would sic their dogs on the black kids or sometimes they would hurl racial remarks and throw rocks at blacks. Orange and blue rebel flags flapped in almost every yard. We made it to Pete's without incident. LaWanda, Angela, and Andrea entered the store while I stood outside guarding the bikes. An older white woman exited the store with a young girl around my age. The young girl had blond hair and blue eyes. They both studied me, then the young girl said, "Mama, why don't the colored girls use their own store?"

"I don't know, Emily. At least this one is dressed halfway decent," the white woman said before they walked away.

I looked at my baby blue dress and leather shoes and was about to smile until I spotted the scuff mark on my shoe. Mama was going to kill me. She had just bought these shoes the week before last. This was only my second time wearing them. I searched the ground frantically for a napkin or something to wipe my shoes off with. Just as I was about to get a napkin I spotted on the ground, Angela, Andrea, and LaWanda came out of the store. Right on their heels was a huge white man with a beet red face and a shaggy red beard. He grabbed Angela and Andrea by the back of their collars. "You black girls are going to jail!" he roared.

Jail? What was he talking 'bout? Another white man, a little smaller than the first and a lot older, appeared in the doorway and grabbed a hold to LaWanda and began pulling her back in the store. I instinctively followed behind him. Where was he taking my sister? Once the first man had come into the store with the twins, the older man holding LaWanda led all of us to the back of the store into a small office. "Okay, you girls empty your pockets," the old man said, pointing a finger at the twins. Neither girl moved. The big man tightened his grip on their collars causing them to wince. The twins stuffed their hands in their pockets and came out with all types of candy. Red Beard let go of their collars and snatched the candy from the twins and placed it on the small metal desk in the office. He then picked up the phone. "I told you, Pa, I seen dem stealing."

"Hold on a minute, Bobby," the old man said, pressing down on the phone receiver.

"But Pa, we need to call the law."

"I'll take care of it. Go watch the store with ya Ma 'fore we get ripped off again."

Bobby left out of the small office, but not before giving us all a nasty glare. Once Bobby was gone, the old man turned to the twins and said, "Ain't ya'll Johnnie Mae's kids?"

"Yes sir," Angela said. Her high yellow complexion was flushed red and she was sniveling. Andrea was right on cue with her sister. I was still confused. Not so much by the fact that the twins had been stealing, but more so because LaWanda was being accused of stealing. Pete had never told her to take anything out of her pockets; besides LaWanda wouldn't steal, we had money. She was still holding our pops in her hand.

"Why are we back here? We didn't steal anything?" I asked. The old man looked at me surprised, as if it was his first time noticing me there. "'Lil girl, I don't know what you're doing here, but these three were stealing," he said, pointing at the twins and LaWanda.

"I didn't steal anything. I paid for these pops.'" LaWanda said, holding up the two pops.

"Yes, you did. I rung you up myself while your two buddies here were stealing the candy for the rest of ya."

"I didn't know they were stealing," LaWanda said.

"Sure you didn't. Anyways, since I know the girls' mother, I'm gonna give you all a break. I'm not going to call the law. I'm going to call ya parents and have dem come pick you up."

Our parents? Did he mean Mama? I'd rather he call the law. I suddenly had the urge to use the bathroom. I mean I really had to go. I know Mama was going to kill us. Worse than that, neither me

## Finding Daddy

nor LaWanda knew Aunt Shirley's phone number. The old man, whose name turned out to be Mr. Pete, called the twins' house and spoke with their dad, who agreed to go next door and fetch my Aunt Shirley. All the thoughts running through my head about what Mama was going to do had my nerves bad. I needed to pee, but Mr. Pete said none of us could leave the room until our parents got there. After about fifteen minutes, there was a knock on the office door and Bobby walked in with Mr. Paul, the twins' father. Right on his heels was Uncle Harvey and Mama. My heart sank and I felt a light stream of urine run down my thigh. Uncle Harvey gave us a look I never saw before. My stomach was in knots. Mama stood next to Uncle Harvey with a deadly look on her face. Once Mr. Pete was done giving his account of what happened, Mr. Paul offered to pay for the items. Uncle Harvey, however, surprised LaWanda and me by saying, "Mr. Pete, I never heard you say my niece took anything. In fact you said she paid for her and her sister's pop."

"Yes, but it's clear they were together," Mr. Pete protested.

"I agree with you, they were together. But I don't believe my niece knew those girls were stealing."

"And tell me, why don't you believe that?" Mr. Pete asked.
"Because she said so. My nieces don't have to steal. You said she had money, yourself."

Mr. Pete had a look of frustration on his face. He raised his arms in the air in a gesture of defeat. "Okay, okay mister. Just take the girls and go, please. I don't want any of 'em back in here again."

When we got back in front of the store, the bicycles were gone. Mr. Paul shrugged his shoulders and promised the twins he would replace the bikes. I couldn't believe it. He was going to buy them some new bikes after they had just been caught stealing. We climbed into the backseat of Uncle Harvey's Benz. I felt the heat from the seat warming my bottom. I wanted to get back to Aunt Shirley's and use the bathroom. Mama sat in the front seat staring out the window as we drove back to Aunt Shirley's. She hadn't said a word. I knew LaWanda and I were in hot water. The only time Mama got quiet like this was when she was mad. The last time she was this quiet, our brother Henry had taken the car in the middle of the night and flattened one of the tires. Mama had to call in to work

~ 13 ~

so she could get the tire fixed. Mama had taken an extension cord to Henry's behind real good. Just thinking about it now gave me goosebumps.

When we got back to Aunt Shirley's, everyone was waiting to lecture us. It seemed like Uncle Harvey was the only one who felt the twins were responsible. I was glad someone had stolen their bikes. Then I remembered that Mr. Paul had promised to buy them new bicycles. I wish I had a daddy like Mr. Paul. I wondered if my daddy had come and got us would he have known, like Uncle Harvey, that it was the twins, and not us, who had been stealing. Mama still hadn't said a word. I had slipped off three times to the lavatory in between being reprimanded. At around dusk, LaWanda and I climbed into the Grenada; we drove the entire way in silence. Mama didn't even turn on the radio and she always rode home from Aunt Shirley's playing the radio and snapping her fingers. I felt sick. LaWanda and I looked at each other. We both knew what was going to happen when we got home. As we eased down Cooney Circle, I felt the urge to use the bathroom again. As Mama turned into the parking lot, the sign that welcomed you to Jennings Homes looked murky under the dim street light.

Once we got in the house, Mama told us to take our bath and get ready for bed. LaWanda and I whispered in our bedroom about who would take their bath first. Neither one of us wanted to be the first to go out the room. I finally surrendered to LaWanda's coaxing, and to my bladder. When I came out of our bedroom, Mama was in the kitchen pouring gin into a glass. She lifted her head to look at me, then quickly looked away and put the cap back on the bottle of gin. By the time LaWanda and I had bathed and put on our night clothes, Mama was tipsy. She appeared in our doorway holding what looked to be a fresh glass filled with gin. "I give you two the world. The world! I'm ashamed of you both, following them fast little girls in that white man's store, got me looking unfit. You won't find a better mother than me. I'm your mother *and* your father!" Mama turned our room light out and walked away, leaving us in darkness.

The next morning Mama woke us early and told us we were going to see Henry. We were both excited. LaWanda ran into the bathroom and began running her bath before I could wipe the sleep out of my eyes. I smelled the scent of bacon and heard Mama

## Finding Daddy

humming in the kitchen. Mama was always in a good mood when we went to see Henry. LaWanda and I ate our breakfast quickly; we were so excited about seeing Henry. I volunteered to wash the dishes even though it was LaWanda's turn. After I finished with the dishes, we all piled into the Grenada. The jail was about forty minutes away from the projects. We had to drive down a long country road with thick green pastures on both sides. Every once in awhile we would see horses and cattle grazing out in the meadows. LaWanda and I sung along with Michael Jackson as he sang "Ben" on the radio. Soon as we saw the jail coming into view, LaWanda and I began giggling. I couldn't wait to see Henry. I looked up to him so much. I didn't care that he had gone to jail. Last time we came to see him, he had promised he would never leave us again.

    We pulled into the jail parking lot and parked as close as we could to the entrance. The sun was hot on our skin as we stepped out the car. No matter how many times we came to the jail, I never got used to seeing the fences with the razor wire coiled around the top. We approached the visitor's entrance and walked into the lobby. The lobby was filled with lockers and small benches. There were also a few public phones mounted to the wall. At the front of the lobby was the registration desk. Sitting behind the desk wearing one of the guard uniforms was the same white lady who was always there to log us in. She sat behind the desk with a condescending look on her face. Mama signed the registration log and handed the woman her I.D. and our birth certificates. The woman took Mama's I.D. and studied it like we weren't just here last week or the week before. She then looked at our birth certificates. "Who is Lucinda Wilson and who is LaWanda Wilson?" the woman asked, looking around Mama where LaWanda and I stood.

    "Why, is there a problem?" Mama asked, before LaWanda or I could answer the woman.

    "No ma'am. I was just wondering because you listed them as your daughters."

    "They are," Mama said, sounding like she was beginning to get agitated.

    "Well, I see you are here to see Henry Bennet, who you have listed as your son. I was just wondering what relation the girls are to Henry? Do they have different daddies?"

"That's none of your business. What *is* your business is to make sure we get logged in and give us our visitor's passes. One thing's for sure, you ain't they Mama. Now can I have our passes, please!"

The white woman's face flushed red. She handed Mama back our birth certificates, her I.D., and three visitor passes. Mama marched us off back toward the lockers so we could put our things inside. The jail didn't allow visitors to wear any jewelry or bring anything into the visiting area except cash for the vending machines. I was still thinking about the exchange between Mama and the woman at the desk. The woman had never said anything about our last names before. It had never occurred to me that Henry having a different last name would make someone think he wasn't our brother. Everybody knew Henry was our brother. My daddy had been his daddy at one time. We were family. Hopefully when we went to court tomorrow, we would all be a family again. Mama said the judge was going to make everything right. Maybe when we come from court tomorrow, we could come back and see Henry again with daddy. Maybe Henry will be able to forgive daddy for their past troubles and we could all be a family again when he came home.

I hated waiting for Henry to come down to the visiting floor because it was always so noisy and crowded. The sound of chairs scraping and babies crying was annoying and it was always so hot. The visiting room had hard surface tables and even harder chairs. I sat at our table while LaWanda and Mama went to get snacks and refreshments from the vending machines. Henry loved the little pizzas you put in the microwave. He always ate about three of them every time we came. LaWanda and I usually ate the hot wings. Mama didn't really like the food from the vending machines; she would eat a bag of popcorn and have a candy bar sometimes.

Henry had gotten so big. I don't know how because he was always complaining about the food when we came to visit. Mama used to tease him saying he was trying to eat everything in the vending machines to avoid the slop they served the prisoners. But it didn't matter, Mama would get him as much food as he wanted from the vending machines.

LaWanda and Mama came back with their arms full of snacks. LaWanda poked me in my side once she placed the snacks

## Finding Daddy

on the table. "Look at Kisha over there," LaWanda said pointing at a table across the room.

Our friend Kisha was at a table with Ms. Pat, her mom and Mr. Tony, Ms. Pat's boyfriend. They lived in the same projects as us. The police had come and took Mr. Tony away a week ago after he had blackened Ms. Pat's eye. Everyone in the projects knew Mr. Tony beat on Ms. Pat. Mama use to say, "I feel sorry for that little girl. No good negro over there beating on that woman in front of that child. They ought to never let him out of jail." Mama was always extra nice to Kisha when she came to the house. Mama couldn't stand Ms. Pat, though. She said any woman that lets a man abuse her or her kids isn't a woman at all. I looked at Kisha sitting at the table and she didn't look happy. I wondered if she longed for her real daddy to come and rescue her. Ms. Pat and Mr. Tony sat holding hands and laughing. Mama looked over at the table and shook her head. "He'll be using her for a punching bag a week after he's out. Here comes your brother."

I quickly forgot about Kisha and all her problems. I looked toward the door that the inmates came out of and seen Henry waiting for the door to open, with a big smile on his face. The door finally opened and he stepped out onto the visiting floor. His blue prison garb was neatly pressed and he had a fresh haircut. He always tried to look his best when we came. Some of the inmates came on the visiting floor looking like they hadn't even brushed their teeth or washed their face. Their uniforms would be stained or in terrible condition with busted seams and torn pockets. Not Henry though, he always looked his best. Even this gloomy atmosphere couldn't dull his gloss.

Henry was always meticulous in his appearance, which was a habit I would learn later on that he adopted from my daddy. Henry reached the table and we stood up to embrace him. The rule on the visiting floor was one kiss and hug at the beginning of the visit and one when it was over. I hated that rule! I didn't understand why I couldn't hug my brother as much as I wanted.

Henry sat down and the smile vanished from his face. "Ya'll like it here? I mean coming to see me here. Maybe you two would just rather be right here with me. Mama out there working hard and you two are out there creating burdens without cause. What were ya'll doing following behind some other girls? Mama didn't raise ya'll to be followers. Look at me. I was out there carrying on thinking I was being a man. Thinking I was easing Mama's load,

but really I made the load heavy. She gotta travel way out here to see me, put money on my books and worst of all she gotta bring my little sisters in this place to see their brother. I went to the chapel yesterday and I listened for the first time. I mean I really listened. You have to learn from my mistakes so that you can be better. When you get home, I want you to read Proverbs 14:24."

Speechless, LaWanda and I looked at our brother. He had never spoken to us like that before. I knew then that Mama had told him all about what happened at the store with the twins yesterday. I felt that feeling from yesterday creeping back up on me. I had disappointed my brother. To me, that was worse than the whuppin' I would've got from Mama. I looked at Mama and she was staring at Henry with a smile on her face. It was more like her entire face was aglow. "When did you start going back to church?" Mama asked Henry.

"Yesterday was the first time since I've been in that I actually went to the chapel, but I've been reading the Bible since the night I got here. I remember you always saying God never forgets us even when we forget him. I feel so alone in here sometimes. I realize all the good things God has placed before me. I'm sorry, Mama."

Both my brother and Mama were teary eyed. I felt my eyes getting watery, even though I didn't understand why I was crying, but I knew something special had just happened between us. LaWanda wiped tears from her eyes. "What does the verse from the bible say?" LaWanda asked.

We all looked at Henry curiously. Mama sat up in her chair listening intently. Henry cleared his throat and looked at LaWanda and me with a serious look. "The crown of the wise is their riches; but the foolishness of fools is folly."

"What does that mean?" I asked.

"It means you can't move through life being thoughtless. You have to think and have foresight on the things that are important. And the servant that knew his Lord's will and prepared not himself, neither went according to his own will, shall be beaten with many stripes."

## Finding Daddy

"Is that in the Bible too?" I asked.

"Yes. That's Luke 12:47. Do you know what that means?" Henry asked.

"I think so. It means we have to always be trying to do the right thing. The things Mama tell us, the things you tell us and the things we know are right," I said.

"And when you don't do those things this is what happens," Henry said, waving his right palm in the air to indicate our surroundings. "These are my stripes for disobeying Mama. You wanna be here?"

LaWanda and I both shook our heads. The huge industry fans they had trying to keep the visiting room cool only managed to toss around warm air. The officers that watched the visiting floor seemed restless as they walked up and down the aisles eyeing the visitors and inmates. I remember thinking, would the C.O.'s receive their stripes for treating my brother less than human?

For the rest of the visit we talked about the good times we had together. Mama had even mentioned a time when we were young and we had all gone on a picnic with daddy. Henry had said he and daddy went fishing that day and he had caught three fish. When the visit was over, we all embraced. Mama told the woman that had logged us in at the lobby to have a nice day on our way out.

When we got back to the projects, Mama let us go outside. LaWanda and I were both surprised, we thought we were going to be on punishment for the next couple of weeks since we had gotten in trouble with the twins. Mama said she was going to make a run to the package store. She told me and LaWanda to be in the house before dark. We ventured out into the Jennings Homes complex searching for our friends. Things were changing in the projects. Some of the older boys had started dealing drugs in the complex and the law was on high alert for any illegal activity around the projects. Some of the older boys had bought nice cars with loud stereo equipment hooked up inside. They rode through the apartment complex blaring loud music and flashing their gold chains and expensive tennis shoes. We ran into Kisha out on Cooney Circle. "Hey Lucinda, LaWanda. Where ya'll going?"

"No where just walking round," LaWanda answered.

"We saw you at the jail with ya mom visiting Mr. Tony.

We was there seeing Henry," I said.

Kisha's face showed surprise. She hadn't even seen us. "Yeah Mama said dem white folks need to stay out of dey business"

LaWanda and I just looked at her. "Is Mr. Tony your daddy?" I asked.

"Yes. I mean he's not my real dad but he's like my dad. He lives with my Mama."

"That doesn't make him your dad just cause he lives with your mom. Where's your real dad at?"

"My real dad left when I was a baby. My Mama said my real daddy is doing twenty years in the state prison for robbery."

"Twenty years?" I asked. "Why don't you go see him?"

"My Mama won't take me to see him. I don't need him anyway. My dad will be home in a few weeks."

It was amazing to me how easily Kisha accepted Mr. Tony as her dad, especially when she knew who her real dad was. Mama never made LaWanda and I call any of her male friends dad, no matter what. I remember one of Mama's friends asked us once how would LaWanda and I like him to be our new daddy. Mama had gone off. She put him out and he never came to our house again. When LaWanda and I used to see him after that, he wouldn't even speak. Mama always used to say our dad may be no good, but he was our dad and, good or bad, he blessed her with us. I started thinking about what was going to happen in court tomorrow. What if our dad still didn't want us? Would I ever have someone to call daddy? LaWanda broke me out of my thoughts. "Hey ya'll let's sneak in the drive in," LaWanda said with a giggle.

A bunch of us project kids use to sneak into the drive in behind the projects. Sometimes we would get chased away by one of the employees. Most times if they did see us they would just smile at our impish behavior. We headed around the back of the projects and as we rounded the corner, we ran into Terell, Larry, and Jimmy. Terell and Larry were cousins. They could've passed for brothers as they were both tall and lanky and wore their hair in dredlocks. Jimmy was fresh home from the state home for boys. He had developed a nice physique in the year he had been gone. He had a neat brush cut and his green eyes were cat-like. "Where

# Finding Daddy

ya'll going?" Jimmy asked.

"We going to the drive in," Kisha nswered. "Ya'll sneaking in?" Larry asked.

"Yes."

"Cool, let's go," Larry said, heading toward the fence that ran along the perimeter of the back of the projects. We all squeezed through the gap in the fence made long ago by the older kids. We eased down the narrow dirt path, careful not to slip on the sward on either side of us. When the path opened up, we saw the screen from the drive in. We had just missed the movie. The credits were rolling as we approached. We decided to wait for the next show. LaWanda, Kisha, and I sat on a log. Kisha started telling us about her new school clothes and then I smelled it. That strong, redolent odor of marajuana. Henry had smoked a couple of times when Mama was at work. He said he would kill LaWanda and I if he ever found out we were smoking. Jimmy had the joint in his mouth sucking in the fumes. I couldn't believe they were smoking. Jimmy offered the joint to us. LaWanda and I declined, but Kisha took the marijuana cigarette. She pulled the joint twice and passed it back to Larry. LaWanda and I gave her a look of disapproval as she exhaled a cloud of smoke.

"I didn't know you smoked," LaWanda said.

Kisha giggled. "Girl, I been smoking for like two years. My dad lets me hit his joints sometimes."

Did she just say her dad let her smoke? How could Mr. Tony let her smoke? I started thinking about our visit earlier with Henry and the things he had said. I thought about what happened with the twins yesterday and I had the sudden urge to go home. I told LaWanda I was leaving. I didn't wait for her to respond I just got up and started making my way back up the path. I knew LaWanda would be right on my heels. If I came home without her, Mama would flip out. Mama always made us stick together. There were times LaWanda would want to go somewhere without me and Mama would say, "If your sister can't go, you don't need to be going." But I was taking the lead today. I wasn't about to let no one else get me in trouble. I hoped Mama didn't smell the odor of the weed on my clothes when I came in. LaWanda and I made our plan on the way back up the path ignoring the calls from Kisha and the others. I could hear Jimmy laughing and calling us square. I didn't

~ 21 ~

care, though. Nana always said, "a square is in good shape compared to a pretzel." LaWanda and I decided to take our baths early and change into our night clothes to avoid taking a chance on Mama smelling the smoke on us. I swore I smelled the smoke in my clothes.

I was so nervous when we got to the back in the complex. We ran into Tiffany; she was one of the older girls in the projects. She was so pretty and she always wore the nicest things. Her hair was always done in a nice style. She was wearing a cute pink Puma track outfit with matching Puma tennis shoes. Her hair was done in Shirley Temple curls and from her ears huge door knocker earrings hung. She smiled as we approached. She was standing with Scooter next to his car. Scooter was Jimmy's older brother. He thought he was God's gift to women with those green eyes. Every time I saw him, he was trying to mack on some female. A couple of the girls in the projects had gotten into fist fights over him. Mama said, "Dem young girls are stupid, out there fighting over a boy that ain't got no plans on being a man anytime soon." I wondered what Tiffany was doing hanging around him. Tiffany waved us over to where they were standing. "Hey ya'll. Where ya'll coming from?"

"We was round back," I said.

"What ya'll doing, sneaking in the drive-in?" Scooter said, laughing.

"No!" I said, snapping my neck and rolling my eyes at him. Tiffany started laughing. "Is ya Mama going to let me do ya'll hair before ya'll go back to school?"

"I don't know. I hope so. Can you do my hair like yours?" I asked with pleading eyes Tiffany reached out and ran some of her fingers through mine and LaWanda's hair. "Yeah, I should be able to hook you up. Ya'll will be so cute with braids, though."

Ms. Parker, the candy lady, called out to Scooter from across the courtyard. She walked briskly across the courtyard heading toward us. "Hey babies," Ms. Parker said as she reached us.

"Hey, Ms. P," LaWanda and I said in unison.

"Hey,Tiff. Looking good as usual."

"Hey, Ms. P. When you gonna have some more hot sausages over there?"

## Finding Daddy

"Girl, I got to go to the market later on today and get some stuff. Hey Scooter, what you got good for me?" Ms. Parker sniffed and smiled.

"What I got is all good, you know that. What you want?"

"Let me get two grams," Ms. Parker said, rubbing a hand across her nose and sniffling. She reached into the front of her dress and pulled out some money. She held the bills pressed tightly between her index finger and thumb. "I hope these bags is bigger than the last ones I got from you."

Scooter laughed and turned to Tiffany. "Go head and hook her up."

Tiffany pulled two folded glassine envelopes from her bra and handed them to Ms. Parker. Ms. Parker examined the envelopes and handed the money in her grip to Tiffany. LaWanda and I looked on. I couldn't believe what I just saw. Mama had been warning us about the drug activity going on in the projects, but we had not been witness to anything like this. I especially didn't know Ms. Parker was involved with drugs. LaWanda and I told Tiffany we would see her later. Just as we were walking away, two police squad cars came speeding into the parking lot. Scooter tried to jump in his car, but it was too late. One of the policemen grabbed him and pushed him to the ground real hard. One of the other officers grabbed Tiffany. She began to struggle and the officer threw her to the ground. People started coming out of the complex into the parking lot and crowding around. More police cars started entering the parking lot. The officers had finally got Tiffany into the back of one of the cruisers. She was yelling and screaming, kicking the glass of the cruiser. I thought for sure the window was going to break. Ms. Parker and Scooter were put in the back of police vehicles as well. Jimmy, Kisha, Terell, and Larry came walking up. "What the hell happened?!" Jimmy yelled. Without waiting for a response, he walked up to the police cruiser Scooter was in. One of the officers pushed him in his chest and told him to step away from the car. Without warning Jimmy swung, hitting the officer square on the chin knocking him out cold. That almost started a riot. One of the cops swung his night stick hitting Jimmy in the back of the head. All the older boys and some parents began to fight with the police. LaWanda and I looked on in disbelief until we felt a strong hand on the backs of our neck.

"What the hell is ya'll doing out here?" We were spun around to a familiar anger that was shocking. Mama stood there in her house coat and slippers. She gave us no chance to respond as she forcibly pushed us away from the melee, directing us with a firm hand on the back of our collars and squeezing her fingers into our shoulders. I winced from the pain and struggled to hear what was going on behind me at the same time. I guess I was suffering from an odd sense of bewilderment. I was curious about all that I had seen and what was going on with Tiffany and the others, but I was terrified at the fact that my mother had discovered LaWanda and I in attendance at such a commotion. Mama wasn't accustomed to drama in her life. Our friends were rarely allowed past our door, unless Mama was home or she really liked you. Her grip pressed into my shoulder all the way to our apartment, possibly leaving an impression.

Our three-bedroom unit was identical to all the other low-income housing structures that made up Jennings Homes, consisting of plain white sheet rock and cheap tile floors. Our kitchen was eight feet by ten feet including the sink, stove, cabinets, refrigerator and counter space. It was about the size of a jail cell according to my brother Henry. The living room was a wide open space as soon as you entered the apartment. A three-piece burgundy furniture set was arranged around a cedar coffee table, our floor model sat against the living room's furthest wall along with the stereo system. A hallway led to our rooms. Henry's room was the first one you came to and LaWanda and I shared the next room which was directly across from the bathroom. Mama's room was at the end of the hallway. When we entered the apartment, a gust of hot air heated my face. Mama finally released her grip on us. "What the hell was ya'll doing out there!" Mama asked, rhetorically. "You don't never stand around trying to see what the hell's going on when it don't concern you. You could've been killed! Get in that room and don't come out for nothing!"

LaWanda and I eased off to our room. We still heard the commotion going on outside but neither of us looked out the window. Like Mama said, it didn't concern us. After about a half hour, it was quiet outside our window. I heard Mama moving things around in the kitchen and the smell of fried chicken made my stomach rumble. "LaWanda are you hungry?" I whispered. She

# Finding Daddy

nodded her head, yes. "Me, too. I hope Mama made some gravy and rice, too."

Mama finally called us to eat. LaWanda and I sat side by side on the loveseat and ate in silence. Mama sat on the couch drinking her gin, the half gallon Seagram's bottle sat at her foot half empty. She occasionally laughed out loud at the antics of Redd Foxx on the T.V. screen. LaWanda and I finished our dinner and prepared to take our baths. Mama was extra tipsy by the time I got out of the tub. The bottle of gin was almost empty and Mama was stretched out on the sofa. The light from the T.V. glowed bright in the dark living room. Our apartment was blistering hot since the cooling system had gone out again. It was the second time this month. I kissed Mama goodnight, tasting the liquor on her lips and went into our room. I had a sleepless night because of the heat and I kept thinking about court date tomorrow. I had looked up the word "paternity" in the dictionary. It gave a few different definitions, but the one that stuck out most to me was, *"ancestry descent from a father whose paternity has not been legally established."* I guess that's why we were going to court, for the man with the wooden hammer to tell us who our father was.

The next morning Mama woke us early. She was already dressed and her bout with the bottle of gin the night before was undetectable in her manner. It was rare that Mama dressed up during the week, but by chance she did, no one would ever think she worked in a factory. Today she was wearing her blue blazer and skirt and a blue and white pinstripe blouse. Her most stylish feature no doubt was the blue kidskin heels on her feet. A breakfast of bacon, eggs, and toast waited for us on the kitchen counter. She told LaWanda and me to put on our best dresses and shoes after we bathed. Our cute little dresses weren't even a shadow to Mama's wardrobe. Mama's face had a glow to it as she moved around the living room straightening up and humming a tune under her breath. Her mood brought a warm feeling to me. I felt like it was going to be a great day. I remember almost losing that feeling once we stepped out of our apartment. Traces of the activities the evening before were still there. I saw pieces of torn garments, a loose tennis shoe, broken glass, and blood stained the pavement in certain areas. As we made our way to the Grenada, Mama shook her head. "These fools done went and tore up their own space." Mama inspected the Grenada on both sides for damage before getting into the car.

    We drove downtown to the courthouse singing at the top of our lungs with the radio. When Mama pulled into the parking lot, I suddenly remembered why we were there and I felt that feeling again. My heart started beating in my ears. I had made up my mind that I was going to speak to my father today. My nerves had my palms sweating and my feet felt heavy as we walked into the courthouse. We entered the same courtroom as before. I looked around searching for that face. I didn't see it anywhere. I did see one familiar face though. The judge sat on the bench looking tired and haggard like he had spent a sleepless night like me. I remember I kept watching the door, waiting for my daddy to come in. My nerves were bad. I didn't think my dad was going to show up. I know he wasn't happy last time we were here. Then he came through the door. Our eyes locked as he came toward us. I thought he was going to come sit right next to me, but he took a seat in the pew across from us. My palms felt real damp and my heart was really beating against my ear drums now. I don't know how I did it, but I raised my little hand and managed a wave. My heart froze for a moment, then my daddy smiled at me and wiggled his fingers in my direction. I couldn't believe it. My daddy had spoken to me, not verbally, but to me it was like he had called my name. I felt Mama pinching the flesh of my leg between the knuckle of her index finger and thumb. "Sit still and look straight," Mama said, in an almost whisper. And just like that, the moment was gone.

    When the judge called our names, we went to the front of the courtroom. The judge shuffled through some papers. He looked up from the papers and glanced at all of us over the rim of the wired frames on his face. He cleared his throat before speaking. "The last time we were here, the court ordered a test to determine paternity in this matter. I have before me the results of that order." The judge paused and looked at our faces again before continuing. "Mr. Wilson, last time we were here you were sure these two young ladies weren't yours. I have you going on record saying so." The judge paused again. "Mr. Wilson let me read you the results of the paternity test. Test results concerning LaWanda Wilson are 98.8 percent positive. The results concerning Lucinda Wilson show 99.9 percent positive in determining paternity. So, Mr. Wilson, I

# Finding Daddy

ask you today again. Are you the father of these two girls?"

There was a long silence, then my daddy looked over at us teary eyed. "Yes, your Honor, those are my girls."

Did he just say we were his girls? I felt like a load had been lifted off my heart. I finally had a daddy, *my* daddy. I was so excited I didn't even hear the judge's order. All I knew was my daddy was back in my life. Mama was happy, too. She was crying and holding us close. When we left the courtroom, we all walked to the parking lot together. Daddy kept apologizing to Mama for putting her through this. Daddy asked Mama if he could spend some time with us. I was hoping Mama said yes. I wanted to spend some time with my daddy. Mama reluctantly agreed to let daddy take us to McDonald's under her supervision, of course. Daddy told us to wait while he went and got his car. I remember standing next to Mama's Grenada in the hot sun. I didn't even feel the heat, I was so excited. Daddy pulled up on us a few minutes later in a shiny black Saab. His car was nicer than my Uncle Harvey's. LaWanda and I got into the car. We both squeezed into the front seat. For a while we drove in silence. I occasionally looked back to see Mama following close behind us. My emotions were in disarray. I was so happy to finally be with my dad, but I was also feeling a little anger. I had so many questions. I wanted to know why he had left us and why he never tried to find us? Did he love us? Was he going to come back and try to make things right with Mama? But for all the questions I had, I couldn't muster the courage to ask any one of them for fear that he may go away again.

We pulled into a McDonald's parking lot and we all got out. I remember it was the very first time I had a Big Mac. Mama never let us order Big Macs. Daddy told us to get whatever we liked. LaWanda ordered a Big Mac, too. "So what ya'll think about me?" Daddy asked.

Without hesitation, I blurted out, "We love you." Mama gave me a strange look but she didn't say anything.

"I love ya'll, too. You know love is a strange emotion. It has a mind of its own and we all think we can control it. I know you are probably wondering why I left if I say I love you. I was dealing with some real serious adult issues and I wasn't prepared to be an adult back then. There are some things even adults can't control and certain circumstances cause us to revert back to our childhood. I'm sorry."

I didn't know why, but I was crying. I thought I saw mama's eyes getting teary as well. After we left McDonald's, we went back to the apartment. The maintenance men had come through and cleaned up the parking lot and sidewalks, but they hadn't fixed the air in our apartment so we all sat outside. Daddy asked us about our grades in school and our regular activities. He told us about North Carolina. He said he would take us there one day. He gave LaWanda and me ten dollars apiece before he left. He promised to call us when he got back to North Carolina. He said he would drive back down and see us every other weekend. Then he left and never called or came back. And just like that, our daddy was gone again.

# CHAPTER 3
## FINDING ME

By the time I was thirteen and a half, Jennings Homes was out of control from all the drug activity. They had even built a police sub division station in the projects. It had little effect on cleaning up the projects and, nonetheless, it was there. Mama was fed up. She said it wasn't even safe for us to play outside anymore. When she said we would be moving, I never thought it would be so soon.

Two weeks after she made the announcement, LaWanda and I were packing our things. We had been invited to Kisha's birthday party the next day.

We had been excited all the way up to the point when LaWanda and I came in the house the evening before when Mama told us to pack. She had said we would be going to our new apartment tomorrow. Her smile was one of gratification, but her joy was lost on LaWanda and I and it must've been apparent on our faces. "Aren't you happy? You'll have your own rooms and the neighborhood is so much better. You'll love it." She said the last part with that confident surety that let us know we had no choice in the matter.

Our fate was sealed. Her decision made. There would be no party tomorrow, just goodbyes. I couldn't believe it. "Where is it Mama? Is it far from here?" I asked, hoping it was within walking distance or on the bus line. This party was my coming out. I was beginning to feel differently.

"Far enough. Well, away from the foolishness that's going on here. I can't raise ladies in this environment. I need to have some place better for Henry to come home to. Don't you want your brother to have a good home to come home to?"

"Yes ma'am," we said. Mama always did that, using Henry as a trump card to get our attention to what she wanted.

I was really looking forward to Kisha's party. The three of us had exchanged friendship bracelets the evening before. You remember, the colorful, rubbery plastic ones everyone used to wear in the eighties. LaWanda and I had all new clothes, too. I was all ready to show off my acid washed jeans and jelly shoes. She said her mother had hired a D.J. to play the music. We were supposed to bust out with this routine in the middle of the party when the D.J. played Run DMC's, "Walk This Way," featuring Aerosmith. We had worked on the routine for two weeks in the privacy provided by the pathway to the drive-in. A couple of times we had to break up our rehearsal to pretend we were just on the path to sneak to the drive-in. I couldn't believe this was happening. "What about school, Mama? If it's far away, how are we going to get to school?" I said, hoping I had thought of something Mama hadn't considered.

"I am going to register you in a new school on Monday. I already called your old school and told them that you would be transferring to another school district. Don't worry, the new school is a lot better. I already checked it out."

A new school district! That meant meeting new people and trying to make new friends. I wasn't up to that. LaWanda and I had already started drifting apart due to our small, but significant, age difference. Mama had started letting LaWanda date and I wasn't always able to tag along with her and the young boys that came trying to court her. Who would I follow behind now when LaWanda disappeared? I was so used to having my own little circle of friends. The boys I beat in foot races and climbing fences in the absence of my sister would be gone, although it had been some time since I had challenged a boy to a race or actually climbed a fence. These things seemed significant at this moment. I was all prepared to express myself as a true individual among my peers and now that was being taken away. I would shut down again in the face of new personalities until I see my likeness in those around me.

LaWanda and I reluctantly packed our things. Mama had given us cardboard boxes and a permanent marker. We packed our things, marking the boxes in accordance with the particular items placed in each box. Mama would tolerate no disorganization. She was, after all, raising ladies. "What do you think this new neighborhood is going to be like?" I asked LaWanda.

## Finding Daddy

"I don't know. I was really tryin' to go to Kisha's party tomorrow. I wanted to rock our routine."

"Yeah. I know. I wanted to wear my new Vanderbuilt jeans and my Reeboks."

"I know, right. I was going to wear the badest outfit," LaWanda said, holding up a Members Only jacket and some acid washed jeans. "Well I guess we'll get to wear our new things at the new schools we go to."

Oh my God! LaWanda had just reminded me of another awful truth. I was still in middle school and she was in high school. We were already going to different schools. But it wasn't such a big deal since I knew most of the kids I went to school with because most of us lived in the projects together. But now, I wouldn't know anyone. The truth of it was, I didn't want to leave the projects.

I didn't want to venture out into a new world, possibly the world Mama always talked about, "the real world." The one where most of this neighborhood's inhabitants feared. So they grew complacent with the meager offerings of the government: food stamps, low income housing, and simple education. But Mama wasn't going to let us end up like these people around here. The ones who didn't desire anything more than what they had. Mama wasn't afraid to work hard and she made sure we understood the importance of working hard, both in school and at home. The "real world" had no place for quitters or the weak. Was I being weak? I placed the last of my things in the final cardboard box.

Our uncles showed up with a moving truck around noon. It was Saturday, September 12, 1985. I'll never forget it. My uncles had started loading the heavier furniture onto the truck. We were bringing the smaller boxes out front. That's when we heard glass breaking and a scream. We looked toward Kisha's unit. The front door was open and Mr. Tony had Ms. Pat pinned against the door choking her. Kisha jumped on Mr. Tony's back and began to claw at his face. "Get off my mother! Get out! Leave us alone!"

Mr. Tony released his grip on Ms. Pat's throat. He flipped Kisha over his back and she hit the pavement hard just outside their door, banging her head. Ms. Pat stumbled to her feet and back inside their house. Mr. Tony was swinging wild blows at Kisha's head as she lay on the ground trying to cover her head with her arms. People had started to come outside to see what was going on. I remember standing there thinking everyone was standing around watching and no one was doing nothing. I felt so angry inside. I wanted to do something, but I couldn't. My uncles had stopped moving the furniture and was directing us back into our house.

What people said happened next none of us saw. LaWanda and I were made to go into Mama's room so we couldn't look out the window. As soon as they closed the door, we heard the sirens. I knew the police would be coming, especially with the new sub division they had built; they always seemed to be lurking around anyway. Mr. Tony would go to jail again, no doubt. Kisha's party will probably be canceled and everyone in the projects would be talking about the beating they took at the hands of Mr. Tony.

We heard more and more sirens coming. Mr. Tony must've started fighting the police. It seemed like we had been in the room forever. I was starting to wonder if we were going to move at all. After some time, things got quiet outside. I heard the voice of my mother talking to my uncles. "Now that just don't make no sense. As much as the police been over here taking him off to jail. They going to take Pat to jail for stabbing him. If a man had been beating one of mines, I would've killed 'em!"

Did I just hear Mama right? Obviously, LaWanda had heard the same thing. We both eased closer to the room door trying to see what else we could hear. "Man, he didn't look too good when they put him in that ambulance," I heard Uncle Harvey say.

"He better hope they take him to Memorial and not that little welfare hospital around here." Uncle Clarence said.

"You know that's where they taking him and from there he going to jail. I wonder who going to look after that girl with her Mama in jail. I'm going to call Pat's Mama and let her know what happened over here. I know she want to go to the hospital and check on her granddaughter. That fool beat that girl bad." Mama's voice got closer as she came toward her bedroom. "Pour me a small shot, Harvey."

LaWanda and I eased away from the door. Mama came in the room and grabbed her big black leather purse. She sifted through its contents and came out with her black address book. "I gotta call Pat's Mama, Ms. Daniels. Tony beat Kisha up pretty bad and Pat stabbed him. Kisha and him went to the hospital and Pat

# Finding Daddy

went to jail."

"You think Kisha is going to be alright?" LaWanda asked, her voice full of concern. Kisha was both of our friend, but she and LaWanda were closer in age and were ultimately closer. They had gone on double dates together and had most the same classes at school.

"She should be fine. Probably bruised for awhile and real sore but she should be alright. It's not life threatening, I'm sure."

"Do you think Ms. Pat is going to get out of jail?" I asked.

"I don't see why not. Them folks know Tony been beating Pat forever. I'm surprised they took her to jail in the first place."

Mama called Ms. Daniels and explained all she knew. After she got off the phone, she walked out the room. We followed her into the empty space that used to be our living room. Our uncles had started moving the furniture again. Mama grabbed a cup, quickly tossed it back, picked up a box, and headed out the door. I went over to inspect the cup and found my suspicions to be confirmed. I smelled the lingering scent of gin in the cup. Mama had started being more tactful at hiding her drinking. She no longer drank in front of LaWanda and me. She would stash her bottles of gin in different little hiding places around the house and she would drink from Styrofoam cups or cups that wouldn't expose her beverage. She would swear to us she hadn't had a drop of liquor, but we would smell the alcohol on her breath. We would sometimes find the bottles of gin stashed around and we would empty the contents out and replace it with water. Sometimes Mama wouldn't say anything, depending on the amount of stash we destroyed. But other times she would go into rants about being grown and able to do what she wanted. We would receive threats and were subjected to verbal abuse.

LaWanda and I began to bring more boxes outside and that feeling of not wanting to leave the projects returned. In spite of what had just happened here, I wanted to stay to be with my friends; to be close to what was familiar. The mystery of what lay ahead didn't have me curious. LaWanda and I began loading the boxes on the truck after my uncles had gotten the furniture on. Our movements were idle. "I don't want to move, 'Wanda. All our friends are around here. Everyone knows us."

"I know. I don't want to move either. I don't care about

having my own room. They probably don't even have a candy lady."

We went back into the house. It was completely empty now. My uncles and Mama were gathered in the kitchen. They all had cups in their hands except my Uncle Clyde. He was holding a Budweiser. "Ya'll done putting those boxes on the truck?" Mama asked.

"Yes ma'am."

"I need ya'll to run down to Gurly's for me and get me some light bulbs."

Mama put her cup on the kitchen counter and fished a ten dollar bill out of her pocketbook. "Get some paper plates, cups, and plastic ware, too, cause we might not be through unpacking tonight and we gotta have something to eat with. I'll probably stop by the supermarket and pick up a pack of pork chops, a bag of potatoes, and a can of corn. We can have some baked potatoes, fried pork chops, and corn. What ya'll think about that?"

"Yes!" I said. Mama knew I loved her pork chops. I reached out and took the ten dollar bill she was holding and headed out the door with LaWanda on my heels. We started heading out of the complex. When we got to the front of the projects, we saw Tyrone and Tony holding up the corner. Tyrone was one of the projects' main drug sellers, but he was smart enough to never keep any of the drugs on him. He always had on the latest fashions with his jewelry. Around this time, four-finger rings were a popular look worn by some of the rappers. Tyrone had four finger- rings on each hand. He waved us over to where they stood.

"Wanda no," I said, under my breath. But it was too late. LaWanda had already wandered off in that direction.

Now, I could've just walked in the other direction toward the store. I already had the money and I'm sure I could've carried the items back on my own. But I had to go with my sister because if anything happened while we were away from each other, we would both be to blame. Although we were growing apart on certain levels, the one thing that remained intact was our sisterly bond. I had to watch my sister's back and she had to watch mine. Tyrone and his friend, Tony, were shady. LaWanda wouldn't dare go near them if Henry was home. I really missed my brother. He always made sure we were safe. I just wish he could do the same

# Finding Daddy

for himself; he was always getting into trouble. It was starting to seem like he spent more time in jail than with us. As I followed behind LaWanda, I imagined Henry popping out and forcing us back in the direction of the store. As we got closer, I took notice to how well kept Tony really was. His Levi's were pressed with a deep crease down the front and the back. His white on white shell top Adidas looked new and had the fat laces that were so popular at the time. His white sweater matched the white Kangol hat on his head and the peach fuzz around his upper lip and chin were neatly trimmed.

I also noticed how much more mature he looked than Tyrone. For an instant, a warm wave swept over my body. Then just like that, it was gone. "Hey Wanda, I see ya'll getting up out of here. Where ya'll moving to?" Tony asked.

"We don't know. My Mama ain't tell us. She said it's far away from here. I'm going to be going to a new school and all."

Tyrone spoke, "You sound sad. You should be happy. Ain't nothing round here. This here a trap. Most of us ain't never going nowhere."

"It don't have to be like that. You can move, too," I said, without thinking. I never spoke to the older boys other than a casual wave or a simple hey. But I just felt compelled to say something to Tyrone at that moment.

"Move? What I want to do that for? I'm living large right here in the projects." Tyrone laughed and gave a look at his homeboy, who laughed, too. "I told your brother Henry I would look out for ya'll while he was gone," said Tony. "Your brother really loves ya'll. I guess my job is over. Ya'll be safe and don't ever come back around here to see how we are doing." Tony smiled one last time, turned his back on us, and began talking to Tyrone like we were no longer standing there.

LaWanda and I turned and started back on our original journey to Gurly's. I thought about what Tony had said: "Be safe and never come back around here to see how we are doing."

He smiled when he had said those things, like he had pride in the fact that he would advance no further in life than the structure of this low-income housing project. Mama was right, I guess. Most of the folks around here really didn't want anything beyond what they had. Hearing Tony made me eager to explore the

~ 35 ~

"real world." I didn't want to think that these projects, the crime that plagued the neighborhood, and the people stranded here long ago in the dilapidated houses we passed on our way to the store were all there was. The houses where the old folks sat on screened-in porches and chewed tobacco and used rusted coffee cans as spittoons, shaking their heads at the generation before them from the safety of their mesh veils.

I knew at that moment there was so much more and I wanted to see it. I was scared, but I was adventurous and the world was a risk worth taking. I was going to be bold, audacious, and daring. I guess today was my coming out after all.

On the way back from the store, my stomach began to cramp real bad. I tried to quicken my pace but each step I took seemed to twist my stomach into a knot. By the time we entered the projects, LaWanda had to take the bag I was carrying and follow behind my steps as I walked. The crimson stain in my white shorts had probably ruined them. Mama and LaWanda had told me this day would come. I felt icky and my stomach was cramping bad, real bad. I was having my first menstrual. Mama was tipsy when we got back and it took her a second to notice the tears of embarrassment rolling down my face as we came through the door. I rushed straight for the bathroom. "Lucinda! What's wrong with you, girl?" I heard Mama coming down the hall to the bathroom behind me. "Lucinda, you hear me talking to you?"

I made it to the bathroom and closed and locked the door behind me. Mama banged on the door, calling my name. I quickly stripped down and jumped in the shower hoping the hot water would wash away my shame. LaWanda must've told Mama what happened because she stopped beating on the door and calling my name. In the absence of Mama's banging and yelling on the door, I realized I didn't have a wash cloth or towel and, even worse, there was no soap. We had packed everything. Just when I was about to panic, I heard someone enter the bathroom. Mama was outside the shower with a towel, wash cloth, and a bar of soap. She handed me the bar of soap and sat the other items on the top of the toilet. She reached into the folds of the towel and pulled out a feminine pad.

"Do you know what to do with this?" Mama asked, holding the pad up.

Although I wasn't sure, I nodded my head yes. Mama said

she'd be back with a fresh set of clothes for me to wear. By the time I finished showering and getting dressed, all the embarrassment I had felt was gone. I stepped out of that bathroom as a young woman.

## CHAPTER 4
### HENRY RECEIVING WISDOM FROM OLD MAN JOE

Henry lay awake in his cell during the early morning hours. He eased off the lumpy stuffed vinyl, which passed for a mattress in the county jail. The vinyl strip lay on top of a cold metal slab that was bolted to the wall and extended outward about two and a half feet and was seven feet in length. The cell itself was a living hell consisting of a six foot by nine foot concrete and steel structure. Henry had gotten used to the living conditions in the county jail.

He was usually asleep this morning but he was restless this now. He had received a letter from Lucinda the day before. Her words had not offered the usual comfort they often did. Lucinda was very upset in her latest correspondence. She had expressed her disappointment in the fact that Henry was always away from them, always getting incarcerated. She had also spoke about the absence of a positive role model in her and LaWanda's life. It really disturbed Henry that his young sister was going through such a difficult growing process. Henry lay staring at the ceiling thinking about his childhood and wondered if the lack of a father or a positive male role model in his life led him down the path he was traveling.

Henry lifted his frame up from the thin strip and stood over the cool metal toilet that was connected to the sink to relieve his bladder. He flushed the toilet and lay back down on his strip. He heard someone cough in the cell next to him then he heard the flick of a cigarette lighter. "Hey Henry, you woke?" A voice asked.

Henry looked in the darkness toward the direction where the voice came from. It was Blind Joe from off the projects. Everybody knew Joe; you couldn't miss him. He had the biggest bifocals in the city. He and old Teresa Norwood had three kids: Little Joe, Amanda, and Petey. Joe stole aluminum and copper and sold it to the junkyards to get his beer and cocaine fix. Joe was a regular here at the county jail just like Henry. Everyone in the projects wondered how Teresa maintained. Between bailing Joe out and replacing things in the house that Joe had stolen to support his habit when he couldn't steal any copper. One would think they would be the roughest looking family in the projects, but Teresa still managed to keep those kids up. Probably with Joe's check with him being declared legally blind and all. "Hey Joe. Yeah, I'm up. What's happenin'?"

"How much time you pulling down this time, young blood?"

"I'm going to draw some prison time out of this one Joe. It's my second drug possession. They trying to give me three years. My lawyer tryin' to get it down to two. I go back to court next week."

"Second offense. You should be able to get the two years. State prison ain't that bad. A lot more movement, better food, and you can probably be able to come out of there with some type of trade. You know Thomas Earl from the projects? He did four years and came home and opened up that landscaping business. He learned everything he knows about landscaping in prison. Before he went to prison, he was a car thief. He came home with that trade and ain't been back since. You gotta decide what you want to do in life. This place is always going to be here. The question is are you going to be here, too?"

"All I want to do is take care of my mother and my sisters."

Joe laughed and coughed. "You can't take care of nobody from in here. You makin' things harder for your mother being in here. Think about it, young blood. Every time you come in here it takes away from your mother on the outside. She has to take care of you and still maintain her responsibilities out there. Life don't stop because we in here. You think you're the only one suffering? Every time I come in here, I lose a part of me. My kids are growing. My woman is out there with no man, tryin' to fulfill her role as a mother and my role as a father. In my sober state, I'm at my best. My only problem is I am struggling from this addiction. I'll be the first to admit I'm an addict. I'm powerless over myself. It's hard,

## Finding Daddy

young blood. But here's something funny: So many addicts don't even know they are sick and how their sickness affects the ones closest to them."

"So why do you keep drinking and smoking?"

"Because I am flawed. Just like many, but my flaws are more difficult to overcome. I didn't have no real role models growing up. I was surrounded by alcoholics and drug users all my life. My father left my mother when I was five. I never seen him again. I don't think my mother ever recovered from him leaving. She started drinking and taking up with different men. Men who didn't really have any concern for me and my siblings. My mother found her solution in the arms of a man that didn't love her, but provided comfort from her pain. It takes a special man to assume the role of a father, especially for kids that aren't his."

The more he listened to Joe talk, the more respect Henry started gaining for him. He had always regarded him as a hype, just another one of the smokers in the projects. But the more he listened, he realized the addicts and the dealers' lives ran almost parallel. It seemed he shared the same disappointments Joe had in life. He hadn't thought about his father in years. His father had left when he was seven and never looked back. The lack of a male role model didn't seem to affect him. But now it was like he had a new revelation. Maybe if his father had been around, he would've had a different upbringing. Sure, his sisters' father, Robert, had been there, but his presence seemed more like the men Joe had said ran in and out of his mother's life when he was younger. He had never felt any genuine love from Robert and he had never developed a love for him either. Henry did acknowledge the fact that he had adopted some of his character from Robert. Just as Joe had absorbed pieces of the mens' character that came in and out of his life. Robert wasn't a heavy drinker. His thing was clothes and appearance. He took careful steps to make sure he was always neat and groomed. Henry remembered the day Robert made him put his own knot in his neck tie one Easter Sunday. They were almost late because he was having so much difficulty with the tie. Robert wouldn't allow his mother to help him. Henry was furious throughout the church service and afterwards, but he never had trouble with a neck tie again. "So do you think if a child grows up with a father, they will turn out better than we have?"

Joe gave a small laugh. "Young blood, I can't say for sure if children with fathers are better off than those without. What I will say is this: The difference between a boy and a man is simple and a boy has to come to know this before he can truly become a man."

"What's that?" Henry asked the old man, bracing himself on his elbows, eager to hear the old hype's next words. He felt drawn in, like a child seeking wisdom from a father.

Joe inhaled his cigarette deeply before dropping the butt on the hard stone floor. He sat up on his slab and crushed the fiery orange ember still glowing on the butt with his big toe. He made his way over to the toilet and relieved himself.

Henry swung his legs off his slab so that he was in a sitting position. "Joe!" Henry whispered loudly enough to echo in the silent cell block. "Hey man, tell me what's your guess." Henry tried to hide the eagerness in his voice. He didn't want this old school hype to think he was asking him to put him down on nothing. Joe talked with better sense than Henry had given him credit for out in the projects. But nonetheless, he was a hype; a hype Henry had served on many occasions.

The commode flushed and Joe grunted as he climbed back onto his slab. "Think about it, young blood. What have you been doing since you been in? Working out and kicking jive with the same 'ole cats from the projects. Now you know I know ya Mama. I watch her make everything happen for you and dem girls. But see you always out there searching, racing time. You have to realize that first." Joe coughed and lit another cigarette. "Then you have to truly know what the difference between a boy and a man is. A boy does what he wants to do and a man does what he has to. Once you realize that, everything else is just life. They havin' eggs for breakfast, don't over sleep, young blood."

Henry sat on his slab staring at the wall between him and Joe until he heard the old hype begin to snore. He finally lay back on his slab, but sleep was a distance away from his thoughts. For the first time, Henry really thought about how his actions were really hurting the ones he loved the most. He also began to think about his dad, which was something he hadn't done in a very long time. He stared at the ceiling until he heard the squeaky wheel of the breakfast cart coming down the tier. He hopped off his slab and banged on the wall to wake Joe up. "Them eggs on they way, old

## Finding Daddy

timer. I know you don't want to miss them."

Joe grunted and hopped up from his slab on weary feet moving toward the bars where the morning meal would be passed through. "Thanks, young blood. I was in the projects with a fifth of E&J and a pocket full of money. I hate dreaming," Joe laughed, fully awake as he heard the cart near his cell.

Henry rinsed off his toothbrush, gargled, and spit in the toilet. He placed his toothbrush back on the metal shelf where convicts kept their personal hygiene items. "You hate dreaming? I love dreaming about anything besides these walls."

"Yeah, but look what happens when you wake up. Dreams are only good if you are in pursuit of dem. Nuthin' comes to a sleeper but a dream. Ain't that right, Officer Gus?" Joe said as he smoothly slid another breakfast tray off the cart to go with the one he already had. The C.O. gave no response as he rushed the trustee along with the breakfast cart.

Henry pulled his tray through the slot in his bars designed for trays to be passed through. "You know, Joe, a lot of the things you say make sense when you think about them."

"Well maybe you should give 'em some thought, young blood. Now, eat your eggs 'fore they get cold."

Henry opened the lid on the Styrofoam tray the breakfast came in. The steam from the eggs lifted upward and his stomach rumbled. The toast and jelly was nice, but what Henry wanted off the tray most of all were the two link sausages. "Hey Joe, I'll give you my toast and jelly for your sausage."

"No problem, young blood. I'll save that toast and jelly 'til later. Never know what these jokers may bring." Joe lifted the lid on the second tray and transferred its contents onto the one he was eating, everything but the links. "Hey young blood, put the toast and jelly in here," Joe said passing the tray through the bars so that Henry could reach it. The exchange was quick and smooth.

"You know, Joe, you alright."

"No I'm not, young blood. I'm away from everything I love. That's what I been tryin' to tell you."

*****

Robert Wilson was a stickler for the extreme discipline the military offered. He had worked his way through the ranks. He was a Sergeant Major in one of the most skilled and obedient security forces in the nation. He took that responsibility seriously. It was apparent in his dress and his manner. He walked with his shoulders straight and his head held high. He had chiseled features and a strong chin. His uniform was always sharp and his shoes polished to perfection. He moved around the huge training ground of Fort Bragg with confidence. Fort Bragg was the major United States Military installation in Cumberland and Hoke counties, North Carolina, U.S., mostly in Fayetteville, but also partly in the town of Spring Lake. It covers over 251 square miles in four counties and Robert Wilson was known in all four. Especially by the women, both on and off post. On post, he was true to his rank, strict and commanding. Off post, his handsome features commanded the attention of many women, even in the midst of his marriage. Infidelity was a silhouette which followed closely to Robert and his nuptials, a curse which had been following him all his life.

Robert's wife Denise willingly accepted the allure of his charming character. She herself had fallen victim to it and still remained very much trapped in Robert's web. She refused to let these other harlots take away her husband. Robert was a good, strong man and a great provider to the girls, Renee and Kim. Renee, Denise's daughter from her first marriage, was twenty. Renee had recently been diagnosed with liver disease. She had pulmonary hypertension of the lungs and had been hospitalized for the last six months. Kim was their thirteen year old daughter, born six months after they had tied the knot. They shared a nice home off post in Hoke county. The house sat on seven acres of land. The property was surrounded by thick forest and a creek that ran a narrow line down the back of the house. Mature pastures surrounded the landscape. On fall mornings, the dew would lift from the pasture and create a smoke screen around the house. Denise would often watch from the kitchen window as she prepared breakfast, knowing that Robert would cut through the fog returning from his morning run. He ran ten miles every morning, waking at four A.M. to perform a light workout before setting out on his run. The heat of this September day was deceiving, though.

It had the humidity of an August afternoon.

Denise moved around restlessly. She walked through the parlor straightening pillow cushions on furniture. She stood in the middle of the parlor floor and gazed at the furniture. The pea green,

# Finding Daddy

laminated, early 19th century furniture sat around a polished chestnut table. The small rat terrier jumped from the top of the couch and ran to Denise's side. The small bells around its collar chimed as the small dog jumped up against Denise's leg. Denise thought about picking the dog up, then changed her mind. The terrier followed close to her heels and headed toward the kitchen. She stopped at the island in the middle of the kitchen, took one of the doggy biscuits from a bowl, and dropped it at her feet.

The dog took the biscuit and scurried off. Denise peeped at her watch. It read 2:45, almost time to pick Kim up from school. She turned the fire down on the stew and headed upstairs to get her car keys. On her way out the door, the phone rang. She reached it just before the answering machine came on. "Hello."

"Hello. May I speak to a Mr. Robert Wilson, please," a sugary female voice requested.

"Mr. Wilson is not in right now. I am Mrs. Wilson, may I take a message?"

There was a pause and Denise heard a sound like someone was shuffling papers. "Yes Mrs. Wilson. Good afternoon. I'm Julie from the accounting office. I was just calling so I could make sure all the information we have on the payee account is correct so we can allocate the benefits correctly."

Denise was confused. What benefits and allocated to whom? "What benefits are these?"

"The benefits for support for your two children." More shuffling papers. "LaWanda and LucindaWilson. Those are your daughters, correct?"

Denise was stunned. She didn't know what to say. Who were LaWanda and Lucinda There had to be some mistake, another Robert Wilson. This woman had the wrong file or something. "What type of support is this exactly?"

"Child support. Court ordered in Augusta, Georgia for the support of the two children, LaWanda and Lucinda Wilson. I'm just trying to confirm that we have all the information correct."

Denise's mind was racing in a thousand different directions.

Child support. So that's why Robert had gone to Georgia a few months back and then again a few weeks ago. She grabbed a pen and a piece of paper. "Okay, what do you want to know?"

By the time Denise got off the phone with the woman from

accounting, she had the names, ages, social security numbers, and addresses of the two girls. She folded the piece of paper and tucked it away in her purse. She went out to her car and paused before sticking the key in the door to unlock it. She braced herself with her hand on the roof of the car. She felt dizzy. She finally managed to get in the car and start it. She drove in a daze. What had Robert done? The secretary had said the girls were fourteen and sixteen. Fourteen. Just a year before Kim was born. How had Robert hidden this from her all this time. She knew about his infidelities. She even knew most of the tramps he took up with, but she never suspected there was another family out there. Not only was there another family out there, but Robert was supporting them. Denise didn't know this woman or her kids, but what she did know was she wasn't about to let them come along and drain them dry. Robert had some serious explaining to do.

She pulled up to the school. Kim was standing in a crowd of girls talking. Denise watched as her daughter approached the car. She looked and moved so much like her father. Her clothes were worn with care and her stride was purposeful and confident. Denise felt her eyes begin to burn, threatening tears at any minute. She couldn't believe Robert had betrayed her like this. Kim got in the car. "Hey Mama, did you stew the rabbit like you said you was?"

"Yes, baby. I think we'll go see your sister today."

Kim's face broke into a smile. "Is daddy going to come with us?"

"No," Denise snapped. "Mama, what's wrong ?"

"Nothing, baby. I'm just tired. I did a lot of cleaning in the house today."

Kim sat back in the seat as Denise put the car in drive and began to pull off. She knew the only time her mother snapped like that was when she was upset with her father. She wondered what he had done this time to upset her. He was always doing something or she was always accusing him of something. She hated when her parents argued. She would hear them yelling through the house all hours of the night. It always seemed to be about another woman. Kim knew that many women found her father attractive. She had been out with him many times and saw how the women fell over him. He was a charmer, no doubt, always smiling and always sharply dressed. Some of the women were from the base, others

## Finding Daddy

were from the surrounding towns. They all knew her mother and knew her dad was married, but that didn't seem to keep them away. Kim promised herself she would never chase behind any man that was married no matter how attractive he was. "Are we going to stop by the house before we go to the hospital? I want to get a jacket. It's always so cold in the hospital."

"Yes. I need to turn that stew off and grab me a sweater. I'll be chilly in there, too." Denise was trying to hold it together as best she could. She needed to see Renee to calm her nerves and clear her head. She wished Renee wasn't sick. Before Renee had gotten ill they would talk for hours about the problems she and Robert were having. Renee loved Robert, but her loyalty was to her mother. She would sit and listen to Denise for hours, complaining and talking about the women in Robert's life. Renee had suggested leaving Robert many times but Denise would never do that. Admit defeat at the hands of one of these floozies? Robert was her man. No matter what type of man he was, he was her man and she loved him unconditionally. Whoever this woman was in Augusta, Georgia would have to take a backseat because there was no way she was letting her have Robert. She didn't consider for one moment the two young girls the woman had mentioned on the phone. Her only concern was keeping Robert in place for her and her two girls.

Denise pulled in front of the house and got out the car leaving the engine running. Kim entered the house right behind her heading to her room to drop off her book bag and grab a spring jacket to put on when they got to the hospital. She hated seeing her sister laying up in that bed all swollen and unable to move. Renee had been her mentor. She taught her so much. Now the doctors were saying they didn't know if Renee was going to make it. She had a rare lung condition and there was a chance she would need a lung transplant. The problem with that was the waiting list was extremely long. There was the chance that Renee could be put on a priority list due to her father's outstanding military record, but the doctors couldn't even be sure if Renee could receive a transplant until they drained the fluid around her lungs. Kim had offered her lung as a possible donor for a transplant once the doctors knew for sure if Renee was eligible for the procedure. She would give her heart if need be. She loved her sister. Family was the most important thing in her life.

Denise turned off the small flame on the pilot heating the stew pot. She walked over to the phone mounted on the kitchen wall and dialed a number. "Sergeant Major Wilson's office may I help you?" It was Gail, Robert's secretary, another one Denise suspected Robert was carrying on an affair with.

"May I speak with Robert," Denise said, with much attitude.

Excuse me? This is Sergeant Major Wilson's office. Who would you like to speak with ma'am?"

Denise couldn't believe this woman was acting so childish. She knew exactly who she was speaking to. She had called this office almost everyday. "Listen here, Gail! Today is not the day. Now connect me to my husband!"

There was a long pause. "I'm sorry, Mrs. Wilson. The Sergeant went over to the N.C.O. Club. I don't expect him back in the office today. Would you like to leave a message?"

"No!" Denise said, slamming down the receiver. Kim met her in the foyer. "We'll go see your sister tomorrow. Something just came up that I have to go handle. The stew is on the stove, help yourself," Denise said, as she breezed by Kim on her way out the door.

Denise got in her car, put it in gear and pulled out tossing loose gravel as she went, heading in the direction of the military base. Sergeant Major Robert Wilson was happy to be out of the heat. He had spent the day running the recruits through the obstacle course then they hit the gun range. He didn't train his recruits like most of the Sergeants, screaming commands and drilling instructions. He screamed the commands, drilled the instructions, ran the miles, completed the obstacle course, and demonstrated proper handling and use of arms. Robert was exhausted. All he wanted to do was enjoy an ice cold Heineken and catch the rest of the game. The Yankees were leading Boston 2-0 in a four game play-off series. The winner would face the Cubs or the Mets. The sportscasters were already predicting a subway series. The Mets were on their way to sweeping Chicago. The club was fairly crowded with most of the officers gathered around one of the two televisions. The polished boards on the wood floor creaked whenever a soldier raised off his heels anticipating a big play. The huge industrial fan blades spun like plane propellers, blowing a

# Finding Daddy

cool breeze throughout the club.

The door to the club opened and Gail walked in. She stood at the doorway briefly searching the room with her eyes. She spotted Sergeant Wilson sitting near one of the televisions. She made her way over to him. Most the officers and soldiers looked up and watched as Gail made her way across the room. It was rare to see a female in the club during a game, especially a playoff series. The club was usually packed with loud, unruly men full of excitement and male testosterone for sport. The kind that made men gaze at the T.V. screen on Sunday afternoons and watch men in tights toss around a pigskin, only looking away to request another cold beer from the kitchen, where the wife is probably preparing dinner. Gail was a twenty-six year old southern belle. She had honey brown skin and a gracious smile. Her auburn hair was pulled back in a neat ponytail. She held her service hat pinned tightly to her ribcage with her right bicep. Her breasts swelled out of her shirt just below her name tag, her pants were starch straight and creased down the middle. Her hips swayed with each step.

Robert spotted Gail heading his way and stood up. He felt a little nervous. Gail walking in here heading straight for him like that, something had to be wrong. He had just left her thirty minutes ago at his office. They had set up a lunch date for the next day. She hadn't said anything when he left. What was she doing here? He moved toward her shortening the space between them.

He met her in the middle of the floor, aware of the few curious eyes which still kept watch on them. "Everything alright?" Robert asked.

Gail nodded. "I just thought I'd come let you know your wife called after you left. She didn't leave a message but it sounded urgent."

"I'll be headed home shortly. She probably wants me to pick something up on the way" Robert said, leading Gail back toward the doors. When they were in front of the club, Gail gave that million dollar smile.

"So, you still going to feed a girl tomorrow, right?"

"Willie's Rib Shack, best B.B.Q. in the Carolinas," Robert said smiling.

"I love ribs. They better be good or else," Gail teased. "Only rib better than these is the one Adam gave Eve."

Gail laughed and said, "Well, Sergeant Major Wilson, I can't wait! Have a good evening."

"Likewise," Robert smiled as he watched Gail walking away. She should be used as a model to recruit more female enlistments. Robert turned to go back in the club and, out of habit, his eyes swept the parking lot where the officers parked. He saw his gray Jaguar shining in the afternoon sun. Just as he reached for the door handle, he saw Denise's red Cadillac pull into the restricted parking space reserved for Lt. Walker. Robert quickly headed toward the parking lot. He reached her car just as she was getting out. He gripped the top of the door with his left hand and blocked her exit with his body. "What are you doing? You gotta get out of this space right now!" Robert said, through clenched teeth.

"Who's that, another tramp with a sweet tooth trying to get close to the candy man?" Denise said, pointing at Gail's back.

Robert didn't even look over his shoulder. "Did you hear me? You are parked in an Officer's personal spot and you are embarrassing me and making a fool of yourself. Now get in the car and go home!"

Denise reached into her purse and pulled out the information she had written down earlier about the girls and their mother. "The only person making a fool of me is you. Damn you, Robert, how could you do this!" Denise shoved the paper in his chest with a hard palm.

The paper hit him in the chest and fell to the ground. Robert let go of the door and bent to pick up the paper. As soon as he looked at the names written on the paper he felt sick. Denise slammed the car door shut and started the ignition. She backed out the space and swung the car away in a fishtail. Robert watched her go and then studied the paper in his hand. LaWanda and Lucinda Wilson...his girls.

# CHAPTER 5
## FINALLY MOVING OUT OF THE PROJECTS

    Moving out of the Jennings Homes was the best thing Mary Wilson could've done. She had moved herself and her two girls, LaWanda and Lucinda, into a nice apartment complex in a working middle class neighborhood. She'd grown fed up living in the low income housing project where most of the residents lived below the poverty line, making the residents nonexistent in an existing society. She refused to raise her girls in that environment. There were no dope addicts and dealer's hanging out on the corners or peddling their poison in the apartments with no regard for the people who lived there. The neighborhood was safe and clean and offered easy access to transportation, shopping, and local eateries. The landscape around the apartments was well tended. The sidewalks were lined with trees and neatly cut hedges. In the furthest east corner was a pool for residents of the apartments to use. The management also provided private parking spaces for its residents. The inside of each unit was equipped with a washer and dryer and air conditioning unit.

    It hadn't taken the girls long to adjust to the new neighborhood. Once they realized there was a pool and found the boutiques and shops a few blocks over, they forgot all about Jennings Homes. Lucinda's biggest complaint was the fact that she had to walk to school. The middle school was only a few blocks away from the apartments and there was no school bus that picked up kids from the apartments who attended. Mary's biggest concern was the time the girls spent at home alone when she was at work. Lucinda spent a lot of her free time with the Korean family that lived next door. They had a daughter who was the same age as Lucinda and a daughter two years younger. Lucinda would spend hours after school at their apartment. She was very fascinated with their culture. When they first moved into the apartment, Lucinda and LaWanda used to think there was a Chinese restaurant in the apartment complex. It took them two days to realize the aromas that had tickled their noses and alerted their stomachs were coming from right next door. The Korean family was very close knit. The mother was a stay-at-home mom, while the father was an active Sergeant in the military. On the surface, they seemed quiet and reserved. But Lucinda always returned from their house with stories of family games she had played or something new she learned about their culture.

Mary wasn't worried too much about Lucinda. Lucinda was doing well academically and running track for the school. Her interest for boys was mild at best. She was more concerned with LaWanda, as she had started dating a lot more. Being the new girl in the neighborhood made her new and interesting to most of the boys. Mary had a strict rule that no one was suppose to be in their apartment when she wasn't home. Mary knew the girls didn't always follow the rule. She had called home from work on a few different occasions and heard people in the background. She didn't say anything because the girls were doing so well. Besides, they were still handling themselves responsibly and maturely. They kept the house clean and did well in school. Mary's concern with LaWanda had all started with the finding of a boy's baseball cap in her room a few days ago. Mary knew she had instilled good values in her girls, but she was also a young girl once. She was well aware of how convincing young boys could be. The baseball cap in LaWanda's room was proof much hadn't changed since she was a young girl. LaWanda had obviously been under the spell of some young boy to have been careless enough to have left the baseball cap out in plain sight on her dresser. Mary knew she had to get her daughter back on track and fast. She didn't want her daughter to make the same mistakes she made when she was young. Boys were so distracting to a young girl trying to achieve goals.

Although her relationship with Robert had left a bitter taste in her mouth for men generally, she didn't discourage the girls from fraternizing with boys. But she kept a strict hold on the activities she allowed them to participate in. Going to the movies, the skating rank, or to a school function like sports games was cool,

## Finding Daddy

but house parties and loitering on the streets was out; so was boys casually hanging out around the house when she was at work. She would confront LaWanda in a direct, non-confrontational manner. She didn't want to risk cutting off that mother/daughter bond she had established with the girls. She needed to keep that intact so the girls always felt confident coming to her with anything. She wanted them to be independent and strong, but she wanted them to know she was there for them if they ran into any bumps in the road. She was well aware of the fact that life threw curves. Robert had been hers. She now moved the men about in her life with a hard hand. Handling them and not allowing any of them to get close to her or her girls. She had allowed Robert to get close to Henry and he had been untrue and abusive.

Mary tied her robe and made her way toward the kitchen. The plush off-white carpet that ran throughout the apartment tickled the bottoms of her feet as she moved about. She reached the kitchen and squatted before the cabinet beneath the sink where she kept the cleaning supplies. She reached around a can of Lysol and a bottle of Windex, snaking her arm around in the darkness of the cabinet until she felt the gallon of gin she had stashed in the back of the cabinet. She set the bottle on the kitchen counter and turned to the refrigerator. She opened the fridge and pulled out a half gallon of grapefruit juice. She needed a drink bad. She had started drinking when the girls were at school or out of the house. She had promised the girls she would cut back. Mary figured if they didn't see her drinking, they would think she had stopped all together. The truth was she hadn't cut back at all and she was still drinking just as much, if not more. With Henry on his way to prison, she was thinking about moving again to a house, which meant working more hours at the job. She was already pulling down twelve hour shifts, five sometimes six days a week. But she really wanted to be in a house and she wanted her girls to live in a house. This apartment was a step up from the projects but it was still not a house.

Mary wanted her daughters to see the strength of a woman firsthand. She wanted to be that living example of a woman being strong and making it without a man in this "man's world." Mary worked side by side with men everyday and carried the same weight as they did. On top of that, she was a single mother. When her daughters did decide to be with a man, she wanted them to be with him because they wanted to be, not because they had to be. She loved Henry with all her heart, but she didn't understand some of the choices he made. She never considered the fact that the absence of a male figure in his life could be playing a role in his decisions. She had been just as stern with Henry as any man could have or would have been. She just prayed the Lord kept her son from harm and returned her to her safely. Hopefully, he returned home with a better head on his shoulders than he went in with. She would be there for him every step of the way. If he needed anything, all he would have to do was ask. She was upset that she was working so many hours. She hadn't been able to go see Henry as much as she would have liked.

Mary took another swig from her glass, savoring the taste of the alcohol as it ran down her throat. She noticed the answering machine's light lit up and pressed the button to hear the messages. Beep, *"Hey LaWanda this is Larry. You still going to the rink Friday night? Call me and let me know. Peace. Oh, did I leave my hat at your house the other night?"* Beep, *Hello. This is Denise Michelle Wilson. The wife of Robert Wilson. I don't know who you are, Mary whatever your last name is because there is only one Mrs. Wilson and that is me. I don't know if you know this, but Robert has two daughters. We have two daughters. One of which is very sick. This is not a good time for our family right now. I ask that you please respect our space."* Beep.

Mary stared at the answering machine. Was she that tipsy?

Had Robert's wife just called her house and left a message on her machine? She looked at her drink, took another gulp, and pressed rewind on the answering machine.

Mary listened to the message five more times and made another drink before she erased the message. She drained the remaining contents in her cup and put away her stash. She walked back to her bedroom and walked into the bathroom, another perk of the new apartment. As she brushed her teeth, she thought about the message. The woman had said Robert had two daughters, one who was very sick. Mary didn't know if she wanted to be upset with the woman for calling her house, or if she should feel sorry for her. Robert obviously hadn't told her a thing about the paternity suit and the ruling by the judge. Still the same old Robert, still

# Finding Daddy

playing with hearts. But had she been talking about two daughters? She had known Robert had married, but she didn't know much about the woman and didn't care to. Now, she wondered how old the girls were? Was Robert really their father? Mary turned the faucet water off and walked back in her room. She laid her uniform across the bed and plugged in the iron.

    Mary was relieved she had heard the message and erased it before the girls heard it. If LaWanda and Lucinda would have heard the message it would have been a whole other issue to deal with besides the ones already before her. She would have her talk with LaWanda tomorrow. It would be Saturday and she would plan a girls' day out with them both, maybe a trip to the mall and get their nails done. But right now she was going to get dressed and stop by Fort Gordon military base before she started her shift. She was sure she could get some information on Robert and these two kids the woman on the phone was talking about. Lucinda had been born at the military hospital and since the judge's ruling, she had been taking the girls there for check ups. Last time she had taken them, the nurse had thought she was the current Mrs. Wilson. Mary was sure she could get some information on the sick girl's medical status. She wanted to make sure of two things: One, she wanted to know if Robert had fathered two more children and two, she wanted to know if the girl the woman had spoken about on the phone wasn't suffering from a hereditary disease inherited from Robert.

    Mary knew she had to change her phone number immediately. She couldn't risk this woman calling and one of the girls answering the phone. There's no telling what she might say. Besides, the girls were getting over the fact that Robert had disappeared from their lives except for the check that came once a month. He had never called or made good on his promise to come back and see them since that day he left after court. Mary began to get upset just thinking about it. Not only had he done her wrong, he was trying to duck out on his responsibilities. Had it not been for that judge and that paternity test, he would've probably never taken responsibility. It seemed Robert had found another victim. Someone else to charm with his handsome good looks and smooth words. Robert was an artist. He could paint a picture so beautifully until you're shipwrecked in paradise. Mary fingered the cap on her dresser she had found in LaWanda's room. She put it in her closet, grabbed her keys, and headed out the door.

*****

Eighties pop culture was happening all around me. Madonna was a "Material Girl," Michael Jackson had the world in a frenzy with his glittering glove and jacket full of zippers, and teens were creating a phenomenon performing dance moves on a card board box on city streets around the country. I was fourteen years old back then. I was into fashion, music videos, and running. All the foot races I ran on the hard pavement of the projects' parking lot against the young boys had prepared me for a transition I never saw coming. My new school had a far better athletics program than my last school. I enjoyed Physical Education not only for the athleticism, but I also met my first mentor there.

Mrs. Woods ran the entire P.E. Department. She was always very encouraging. She had told me to try out for the varsity girls' track team. Once I got on the track team, I saw another side to her. She would sit the girls around after practice and talk to us, giving enlightenment. She sounded like Mama sometimes when she talked about the struggles we would encounter in the world as women. I was always very attentive when she spoke. Her voice had strength and she was very articulate. She was very forthcoming with us about her life struggles and triumphs. She said she had grown up in New York. She and her first husband had gone to N.Y.U. She started out teaching Physical Ed. at a high school in New York, but once her daughter was born (a product of her first marriage) she decided to move to Georgia. She said she wanted to own something, really start building something as a family. But her husband didn't mind the congestion in the city and he didn't like the pace of Georgia, so he moved back north a year later.

She said it had been hard at first with just her alone trying to work and take care of her daughter. Her first husband provided little to no help with paying the bills or taking care of their daughter. She had made it through by the grace of God and her strong will.

She encouraged us to give our all at everything we did in life, and I tried my best to please her. I was the star runner on our team and I was ranked No. 3 out of all the middle schools in Richmond County. Running track made me start paying more attention to my physical features. I began to apply cocoa butter to the old scars I had gotten from my days in the projects climbing fences and trees.

Mrs. Woods had bought me a huge jar of shea butter and told me to start using it. I haven't stopped since. I loved when we went to other schools to compete. Mrs. Woods would bring her cassette player on the bus and we would sing along with her DeBarge cassette. I loved that song, "Love Me in a Special Way," and for some reason every time I heard it, I thought about my father. I listen to the words of the song now and still smile thinking about those times on the bus and having thoughts of my dad.

My athletic and academic achievements didn't go unnoticed. I was well known and liked by all the school's faculty and my cool demeanor allowed me to meet friends easily. All my uncertainties about fitting in when I had first arrived were gone. I was fitting in just fine. My popularity came with a price though. There was a girl named Sharmaine Johnson. She thought she was the prettiest girl in the school, and often said so. She was a very pretty girl, but her nasty attitude stole away all her beauty. She really hated me and I really didn't know why. I had never done anything to her. I always spoke to her with respect but whenever she came around, she made it her business to try and show me up in some kind of way. I guess she didn't like all the attention I got around the school, especially with me only being there six months. My name appeared in the school paper at least twice a week for my academic achievements and whenever we had a track meet, you can guarantee there would be a picture of me breaking the ribbon at the finish line.

The tension became so thick between us, I knew for sure before the end of the school year we would lock horns. I had already told Mama about the rivalry. Mama told me to avoid trouble but don't run from it. Even Mrs. Woods had pulled me aside and asked me if I wanted her to speak with Sharmaine. Obviously, our rivalry was no secret around the school and like all childhood tug of wars, people choose sides. In hindsight, it was a really immature situation. I wasn't even campaigning for popularity. I just wanted to bring straight A's home to my mom and run track. I wonder what ever happened to Sharmaine? I remember one day after school she and two of her cronies followed me all the way home from school. I remember walking ahead of them. I kept the same pace I always did when I walked home. I wasn't looking for trouble but I wasn't running from it. The trio followed behind me snickering and making off handed remarks indirectly aimed at me. I walked paying them no mind. My right hand gripped the straps of my book bag which dangled loosely at my side. I was confident that I could swing the weight of the hard covered books I had stored in the bag with enough force to knock anyone of the girls silly if they decided they wanted to taunt me with anything more than words.

I had also learned two very important things from Mama and Mrs. Woods that helped me in this situation. I thought about their words as I walked with the trio cackling at my heels. *"If you throw seeds to birds, they will peck at your feet.'"* That was Mrs. Woods. I smiled to myself as I thought about it and listened to Sharmaine and her friends nagging for my attention. *"Never let your shoulders sag in the face of adversity."* Now, that was Mama. I wasn't exactly sure if this was adversity, but I was sure to walk with my shoulders squared and my head held high. Sharmaine and her friends followed me all the way to the entrance to our apartment. They gathered on the sidewalk as I passed through the gate. I turned to them as they stood there looking at me. "Thank you for escorting me home," I said with a smile and turned and walked to our apartment. The next day at school Sharmaine and her two friends avoided me as much as possible. But our rivalry was far from over.

When I wasn't at practice or out competing, I spent most my time with the Korean family next door. I loved spending time at the Yums' home. The father was serving at the same military base LaWanda and I went to get our medical and dental check ups. They had been in Hawaii before he had gotten stationed at Fort Gordon. Mrs. Yums was very short, maybe '4 9," and Mr. Yums wasn't much taller than me at '5 7." I was just a few inches shorter and sprouting up by the second. I went to school with their two daughters Michelle and Julie. Michelle and I were the same age and shared two classes. Julie was a year younger and in the seventh grade. They were both honor students like me and we often studied together. I remember them being great at math. They helped me grasp the concept of algebra in three hours. Besides the hours we spent studying together, they allowed me to be included in their

# Finding Daddy

family activities. They lived very differently in their home than they did at school. For instance, they were called by their Korean names by their parents.

    Their entire home was decorated with cultural items that reflected their heritage. It was awesome. They had beautiful Korean art on the walls of the living room. Mrs. Yums had taken my hand the first time I entered their home and explained each painting to me. All the art had significant meaning to life in their culture. She explained that most Korean artists had traveled abroad to study the works of those considered the masters. In the fourth century, China, as well as many other Asian countries under it's influence, considered itself to be the center of the universe. As such, many Korean painters were sent to China to learn modern Chinese painting styles. What they learned not only influenced Korea, but also Japan as many Koreans migrated to Japan. The hand woven carpets on the floor depicted Korean warriors in traditional medieval dress on horseback. Mrs. Yums explained these were images of The Kaya Federation. The Kaya Federation was a federation of independent city-states in the Three Kingdoms period (the kingdoms in that time period were Koguryo, Paekchae, and Shilla). But they didn't last very long before their stronger neighbors absorbed them into their territory. I was really amazed at the waterfall mural they had built in the center of their living room. It had marble flooring on the inside in the symbol of the Ying and the Yang, a symbol of their practice in Taoism, a religion that influenced Eastern Asia for more than two thousand years. The outside of the fountain-like waterfall was carefully carved granite bricks. It was so peaceful and serene, one would immediately feel welcomed. That little tour would earn me an A on a social studies paper I had to write on the Unified Kingdom of Shilla.

    Their energy was so positive it felt surreal. I always felt comfortable in their presence. I would sometimes walk out of their apartment and have to snap back to the realities of the real world. Their home was so tranquil I would sometimes forget they lived in an apartment identical to ours. I grew very close to them. Mrs. Yums allowed me to watch her in the kitchen as she prepared traditional Korean cuisine. Like most Asian countries, Korean dishes were mostly prepared with rice, but Mrs. Yums did utilize noodles with a lot of her dishes. What I remember most was her constant use of the same ingredients to give the food its flavor. Mrs. Yums had said it was the most important part of preparing traditional Korean food. I still remember the seasonings to this day. She used these same ingredients almost every time she entered the kitchen: sesame seeds, garlic, ginger, spring onion, sesame oil DoenJang (된장, fermented bean paste). Tonight she was making Bulgogi which is the main meat dish among the Koreans. It is also one of the most popular grilled beef dishes in Korea. It is made from prime cut beef and usually marinated with a mixture of soy sauce, sesame oil, pear juice, balce pepper, garlic, onion, spring onion, wine, salt and sugar. Traditionally, bulgogi is usually served with lettuce which is used to wrap the slice of the cooked meat along with some special sauce, rice and other side dishes and eaten as a whole, almost like a taco.

    I waited until we were all around the table eating and then I just came out with it. The question I had wanted to ask since I met them. "Why don't Michelle and Julie use their Korean given names at school?"

    Mr. Yums tapped the corners of his mouth with his napkin and fixed me with a serious stare. Michelle, Julie, and Mrs. Yums all looked at me. I felt my palms begin to sweat in the short seconds that passed since I asked the question and the silence that followed. Had I offended them? "They do use their Korean given names in school. I know because I named them." Mr. Yums began to smile, then Michelle, Julie, and Mrs. Yums began to laugh.

    It took me a second to catch Mr. Yums humor. "I meant why didn't they use the names you use here at the house for them in school?"

    "I know what you meant," Mr. Yums said with a smile. "There are two reasons they don't use Eun Ju and Hye Su in school. The first reason is because it is their middle names. The second and most important reason is because the veil that is discrimination in this country. Just like your people, Koreans face racism and discrimination. I want my children to have the same opportunities as any other citizen of this country. In truth, my children and many other children of minority ethnic groups who live in this country will suffer countless encounters of discrimination in this society. I don't want their names to hinder them as well. If a person can't get

# Finding Daddy

past the name, they'll never get to the person."

Mr. Yums said it was a common practice among Asians living in this country to give their kids traditional American names. It made a lot of sense after he really explained it. He surprised me with his knowledge of Malcolm X and Marcus Garvey. He explained that blacks in this country will always be in an ongoing civil war with the powers that be in this country. He said the Declaration of Independence was actually a meeting held by the Continental Congress, who announced that the thirteen colonies of America were severing ties with the British Empire, as they were engaged in a war with Great Britain. The same year the introduction of a paper monetary system was brought in. This system was designed to determine independence, and still does to this day, rich or poor. His ideology made a lot of sense on the surface, and it caused me to give a lot more thought to the things my mother talked to me and LaWanda about all the time. Mama stressed the importance of making and saving money. That's why she worked so hard, so that she could open doors for herself and us as well. She always said money makes the world go round. I guess she had a point.

I learned a lot hanging out with the Yums. We did a lot of things together too. The one thing I always noticed when I was around them was their strong family bond. They seemed like the perfect family. I felt special being allowed to be part of their family. When I told them Mama was thinking about moving again, we all cried together. Mrs. Yums had said she wished I was her daughter. I looked around at all their faces and thought about all the good times we had together as a family and for an instant, I wished I was their daughter, too. It would be nine months before we moved and I tried to spend every day of those nine months with the Yums. We stayed close for years after we had moved away from the apartments. I lost contact with them when Mr. Yums got stationed in Rhode Island.

# CHAPTER 6
## BEAT DOWN AT THE SKATING RINK

    LaWanda and Toya paid their fare and walked to the back of the bus giddily carrying their bags. They had been in the mall for the last four hours, mostly just hanging out, but they had managed to buy some new outfits to go to the skating rink tonight. Larry was supposed to get his brother's car tonight and drive them to the rink. She had been dating Larry for the past four months. He was a senior and a star running back on the high school football team. He had pursued LaWanda from the moment she arrived at the school. He was smart, cute, and charming. LaWanda loved his smooth peanut butter complexion and the way the dimples formed in his cheeks when he smiled. He was a little short for her taste at '5 7," but his personality and charm made up for his short stature. Besides, he was one of the best dressed kids at the school. His brother drove him to school everyday in his new Volkswagon Rabbitt. But tonight it would be Larry driving the car, and LaWanda was going to be riding shotgun.
    LaWanda was so excited about pulling up to the rink in the car tonight. She knew everybody from school would be talking about her in school on Monday. She had bought the perfect outfit, too. She had brought some Gloria Vanderbuilt stretch jeans, a cute beige halter top, and some beige Kenneth Cole sling back pumps. She was going to be the hottest girl at the rink tonight. She had gotten her hair, feet, and nails done. She couldn't wait until they pulled up in front of the rink and she and Toya stepped out like stars. She hoped Courtney Reynolds was out front when they pulled up. Courtney had been her rival since she had arrived at the high school. LaWanda didn't understand why the girl had it in so hard for her, especially since Courtney was a senior, supposedly on her way to some prestigious university up north. She was dating Carl Simmons, the high school's star forward for the basketball

team. There were rumors he was going to be recruited by Georgia State but those were just rumors, like Courtney going away to some big university after graduation. LaWanda was going to show Courtney tonight.

    Larry said he was going to bring his cousin along after being at the rink. They were all supposed to go to some party across town. Toya told her mother that she would be staying at LaWandas' house overnight to avoid her curfew. LaWanda didn't really have a curfew since her mother worked the graveyard shift; she and Lucinda were able to hangout at night if they chose. Lucinda spent most of her evenings at the Yums.

    LaWanda usually entertained her friends at their apartment while Mary was at work. LaWanda had worked out a deal with Lucinda to ensure she wouldn't blow the whistle on her. The deal was simple: LaWanda would handle all the chores in the house, both hers and Lucinda's. There would never be any traces of her activities from the night before by the time her mother got home. The apartment would be spotless and she would be preparing to leave for school by the time her mother turned her key in the lock. A few nights ago she and Larry had been in the apartment alone. They had been watching T.V. and eating some fried chicken wings when Larry had suddenly kissed her. They had kissed before but this was different, their tongues wrestled passionately. His mouth felt warm and his tongue was electric, sending warm signals throughout her body. They moved from the living room to her bedroom and were making out hot and heavy when LaWanda heard someone come in the apartment. Lucinda had called out to her. LaWanda hurriedly straightened her clothes and met LaWanda in the hallway right outside her door. LaWanda had been so nervous that she barely heard the story Lucinda was telling about the three girls who had followed her home from school.

    LaWanda had managed to get her hormones under control and Larry out the house without too much third degree from Lucinda. Of course, she did have a million questions as to why Larry had been in her room. LaWanda had avoided most of the grilling by getting in the shower, a cold shower that did very little to cool off her raging hormones. LaWanda had lay in bed all night thinking about what had almost happened. She hadn't actually gone all the way with any boys. She had done her share of making out

## Finding Daddy

and petting, but she hadn't actually gone all the way. She hadn't found anyone she felt was worthy of her virginity, until now. She really felt like Larry was the one. He was so kind and caring. His touch made her hot. All the warnings Mary had given her about how boys would work hand and glove to get in a female's pants meant nothing. LaWanda knew Larry wasn't like that. He loved her and she loved him. Her mind was made up.

They got off at the bus stop a block away from LaWanda's house and began to walk. "Damn girl, you walking with so much purpose," Toya said, attempting to keep step with LaWanda.

"Umm, girl you just don't know," LaWanda smiled, and winked her eye.

"Oh really? So you never did tell me what happened the other night between you and Larry, girl. I know ya'll was at your house alone. He didn't try nothing?" Toya eyed LaWanda with a suspicious look and smile.

"Yeah, we were alone for awhile and then Lucinda decided to come home. Girl, if she hadn't come home umm... umm... umm."

"Yeah right, girl. You wasn't going to do nothing," Toya said, with a laugh.

LaWanda didn't respond right away. "So have you ever done it? "Done what?"

LaWanda stopped walking and fixed Toya with a stare. She knew Toya was very flirtatious, but what she didn't know is if Toya had actually done the "do." "Girl, stop playing you know what I'm talking about."

Toya smiled. "Twice."

LaWanda looked surprised. "Twice!" "Yeah. Twice."

"Yeah right, girl. I don't believe you. With who?" "Nobody you know and definitely no one at school." "Yeah right, girl. You are such a liar."

"I'm not lying, girl. You just jealous," Toya laughed.

LaWanda laughed. "For real, girl, who was it?"

"A guy named Abdul from New York. I met him last summer when I was up in Atlanta visiting my cousin Sheila."

Toya continued, "I met him down in Five Points. He was so fine, girl. He had short, wavy hair, chinky eyes and his smile, Mmmm. He looked just like one of those rappers, I'm telling you.

He had the gold chains and the gear. He was so cool. I loved his accent, too. We stayed in a motel for two days."

"Two days! And ya'll only did it twice, yeah right." LaWanda didn't believe her. If it was one thing Mama had said about boys that LaWanda believed was that guys never got enough.

"I'm telling the truth, girl. The first night we didn't even do nothing. His friend was in the room with us. The next day I introduced his friend to Sheila and it was the bomb. They took us out to eat and to the movies, then we went and got a room."

"All four of ya'll was in the same room?"

"No way, girl! We got our own room. It was so fly. The room had a jacuzzi and a balcony."

"Forget the room. How was it? Did it hurt?"

Toya lifted her head to the sky and twisted her neck to the left. "Like hell,girl, at first. But then I got use to it. Umm, just thinking about it," Toya said with a shiver.

"So what happened with you and Abdul?"

"He went back to New York, I guess."

"You guess. What do you mean you guess?"

"Well, it wasn't like we were going out. He was in Atlanta for a weekend. I was there for summer vacation. It was a booty call, girl, and I feel no shame and I got no complaints."

A booty call. LaWanda couldn't believe Toya had just said she was content with being a booty call. LaWanda would never sleep with someone because they were fine or had an accent. Larry was definitely fine, but there was no way LaWanda would even consider giving him her virginity if she didn't love him. Toya had given her virginity to a virtual stranger.

LaWanda opened the door to the apartment. She was still feeling the butterflies in her stomach from the anticipation of what could be tonight. Toya's tale hadn't discouraged her. It just gave her something to think about and her brain was racing. She allowed Toya to take her shower first while she straightened up the house. She wanted to make sure the house was clean when she left just in case she had a long night. She walked into her room and stopped dead in her tracks. Larry's hat was gone from the spot she'd had it sitting on her dresser. She began to look around the room, under the bed, in the closet, in her dresser drawers. The hat was no where to be found. Next, she went into Lucinda's room to continue her

## Finding Daddy

search. She was in the kitchen when Toya came walking out in her new outfit. Toya had on a tight black catsuit and an open toe Nine West pump. LaWanda stopped her search to acknowledge Toya. "Damn girl, we going to be looking hot tonight at the rink."

Toya smiled and did a full spin. "I know, girl. Did you call Larry yet to see if he was still going to be able to get the car?"

LaWanda was back looking through the kitchen cabinets. She knew the cap wasn't in any of the cupboards but she had no idea where else it could be. "Girl, did you call Larry?" Toya asked again.

"Huh. Oh, no, girl, I'm going to call, but I know he coming." "How you know that, you promised him some nookie?" Toya said laughing.

LaWanda laughed. "No!"

"Well, that's the only way you know he's definitely coming. What are you looking for anyway?" Toya said, picking up the liter of gin LaWanda had sat on the counter. "Girl, let's take a shot of this."

LaWanda eyed the gin bottle. She didn't really drink. She had taken a swig or two before out of curiosity, and she didn't particularly like the taste of gin. But for some reason having a drink right now didn't seem like a bad idea. LaWanda got two cups out the cupboard and took the grapefruit juice from the refrigerator. She poured three fingers in each cup and added grapefruit juice like she had seen Mary do so many times before. Toya took the cup LaWanda was offering and drank half the contents of her cup. LaWanda took a gulp and sat the cup on the counter. "I can't believe I can't find my cap."

"Cap. What you need a cap for?" "Larry gave it to me."

"So what, girl. I know you ain't wasting your time looking for no cap when we are about to shut the rink down tonight!"

"I just want to find it, in case he asks about it."

"Girl, if Larry see you in that outfit tonight and ask you about that cap, you need to cut him off."

LaWanda smiled. "I know that's right, girl."

"I just hope I didn't get dressed up for nothing. I'm telling you right now if his cousin is not cute, I'm not hanging around him when we get in the rink. Sorry girl, I gotta go back to school on Monday. I got an image girl, you know that."

"Girl, you are a mess."

"No. I'm honest. I hope no one gets offended if I have to tell the ugly truth." Toya laughed hysterically, picked up her cup and downed the rest of her drink. "Can I have another?" Toya said holding up her empty cup.

LaWanda smiled and shook her head. "Girl, you gonna be stumbling around the rink parking lot. Here finish mine," LaWanda said passing Toya her cup. "I'm going to go get in the shower."

"Wait, why don't you call Larry first and see what's up. We might have to get another ride. I am not getting off the bus in this outfit; it will ruin my whole look."

"Girl, he coming trust me. If Lucinda comes home while I'm in the shower ask her did she take a cap out of my room."

Toya shook her head. "That boy got you all messed up in the head."

"Whatever!" LaWanda said over her shoulder as she walked toward her bedroom. She looked around for the cap again while she got her shower items together. She had no idea what could have happened to the cap. She was sure she had left it right on her dresser, in fact she was more than sure. She had tried the cap on in her dresser mirror earlier that day. She had to find that cap. She grabbed her things and headed to the shower.

Toya was back in the kitchen again mixing another drink when the phone rang. She called out and got no response. She answered the phone on the third ring. "Hello."

"Hello. Who is this?"

The voice on the phone had a belligerent air about it. Toya was feeling a little tipsy and responded to the voice on the phone without realizing she was answering her friend's phone. "Dis is Toya, who dis?" Toya said in a heated tone.

"Toya. Well, Toya this is Denise Wilson. I know what you are trying to pull and it's not going to work. Robert does not love you or your children. He is a very, very happily married man with his own family. You little heifers need to stop messing with other women's men and then try to trap them with some kid. I'm going to make it my business to make sure you don't get one more red cent out of my husband's money for those kids of yours!"

Toya was really fueled up off the gin now. She wasn't even sure what the woman was talking about but she didn't like her tone.

## Finding Daddy

"If you was handlin' ya business, ya man wouldn't be chasing behind me, trick!" Toya slammed the phone down not waiting for the woman to respond.

LaWanda unwrapped the towel on her head and dabbed at the moisture that was still around her shoulders and neck. She was fresh out of the shower. Her body felt warm all over and her heart was racing. She was excited about the fact that she had made her first adult decision. Tonight she had decided to give Larry her virginity. They shared so many interests and most importantly she was sure he loved her. He had been so patient; Larry was different. He saw inside to the real her. He wasn't just trying to score with her and LaWanda knew it. She knew Larry loved her. LaWanda got dressed and walked out to the living room. Toya had her head tilted back and her cup glued to her lips. "Who was that who called?"

Toya took the cup away from her mouth long enough to mumble, "Wrong number."

"Oh. So girl, how do I look?" LaWanda did a full spin and bent her knees in a bow.

"Like the queen of sexy. I can't wait to step up in the rink tonight."

"Girl, I'm gonna make Courtney look so uhg!" LaWanda said, sticking her index finger in her mouth in a gesture like she was going to make herself vomit.

The phone rang again and Toya rushed to pick it up. Not knowing if it was the same woman who had just called. She didn't want LaWanda to get the phone and find out what she had just done. "Hello."

"Hey Lucinda, your sister round?"

"This is not Lucinda. This is Toya. What's up, Larry?" Toya looked at LaWanda and winked. LaWanda started walking toward her cheesing.

"Hey, hey, Toya?" Larry said with a laugh. "Where's my baby at?"

"Your baby?! Umm. I heard that. She right here." LaWanda reached for the phone but Toya pushed her hand away and signaled with her index for LaWanda to wait a minute. "More importantly, where you at? Were you able to get the car ? And where is your cousin and know if he ain't cute he will be getting no play with

~ 69 ~

this."

"Girl, you crazy. Yes, I got the car and I'll be there in like twenty minutes. Make sure ya'll are ready. Now put my baby on the phone."

"What about your cousin?"

"Girl, put LaWanda on the phone."

Toya reluctantly passed LaWanda the phone. "Hey." LaWanda said in a sugary tone.

"Hey what's going on, baby, you about ready?" "Yeah, we ready. Where you at?"

"I'll be there in about twenty minutes. We had to make a quick stop."

LaWanda heard a lot of noise in the background, muffled voices and music. Toya kept telling LaWanda to ask about his cousin. LaWanda finally walked away from Toya waving her off. "What's all that noise in the background?"

"I'm over here at my aunt's house in the projects; my cousin had to drop something off. So you going to be looking good for me tonight?"

LaWanda felt herself blushing. "Yes, you already know."

"I got a little surprise for you later. Where do you want to go to eat?"

"It ain't going to be that many choices for food by the time the rink close. I guess we'll just hit the Waffle House up. So, what's my surprise?"

"I can't tell you that."

LaWanda smiled. "I got a surprise for you, too." "Really, what's that?"

"I can't tell you either. I guess we'll both be filled with anticipation until one of us exposes their hand."

"Oh, so that's how you want to be, huh? Alright." "I'm just following your lead."

Larry laughed. "My lead, okay then just don't lose step." "Never."

"That's what I'm talking about. We about to leave from over here. I'll be there in a minute."

"Okay, baby." "I love you."

" I love you more." LaWanda hung the phone up and took a deep breath. She exhaled, trying to let go of all her insecurities and

## Finding Daddy

doubts. She wanted tonight to be perfect. First, she wanted to show Courtney up, and then top the night off by giving her virginity to Larry. LaWanda turned around and caught Toya staring at her shaking her head. "What?"

"Girl, you sprung."

"Like a spring," LaWanda laughed.

"So what's up with his cousin? Is he with him?'

"Yes girl, yes. You talking about me being sprung... you ain't even met the cousin yet and you can't stop talking about him," LaWanda laughed.

"I just want to make sure everything is everything." "I'm sure. So do you think about Abdul still ?"

Toya took in a breath. "All the time, especially late nights," Toya said, laughing.

"So, why didn't you ever do it again?"

"I told you he went back to New York."

"I'm not talking about with him. I mean why haven't you had sex again?"

"Well, besides the fact that I really haven't found anybody I'm ready to get with like that. Most of these dudes talk too much. You give them a little nookie and the next thing you know, all their boys will know. Some guys talk more than women. You thinking about giving Larry some ain't you?"

"No,"LaWanda said too quickly and then broke out into a huge grin. "Well, maybe girl. I really care about him, and he feels the same about me. I really want to do it. You think I should wait?" "Girl, I can't begin to tell you what to do. This isn't an issue you really take advice from a friend on. This has to be all on you because no one can live with the regret but you if there is any. I went with my gut when I gave up my virginity. I don't have any regrets, not even that I may never see Abdul again. I wouldn't change that experience for the world, but that's just me. You and I are two different people. Only you can make a decision like that. But I do appreciate you asking me, it shows you really trust my judgment as your friend. Thank you."

"You know you my girl. I don't know what else the night is going to bring but I hope whatever happens it's special because that's how I'm feeling tonight."

"I'll drink to that," Toya said heading back toward the

~ 71 ~

kitchen. LaWanda followed behind her and stopped dead in her tracks when she saw the gin bottle on the kitchen counter. The bottle was more than half gone. "Damn, girl, you drink just as much as my Mama. We going to have to get another bottle. My Mama is going to straight trip if she come in here and see this bottle like this. You think you can get your brother to buy us another bottle and we pick it up on the way to the rink?"

"Yeah. He'll do it. Let me call him real quick," Toya said adding a little grapefruit juice to the gin in her cup.

LaWanda went in her room and opened her jewelry box. She pulled out her money and counted it. She had $197 which was what she had left over from the check she received from her father. She and Lucinda both received a separate check from their dad every month for four hundred dollars. Mary still took care of most of their needs so the girls were allowed to spend the money any way they saw fit. The only catch was if they spent the money before another check came in they would be broke. Another one of Mary's little life lessons. LaWanda counted out $67.00 and returned the rest of her money to her jewelry box. She grabbed her jacket, turned off her room light, and walked back out to the living room. Toya was turning up her cup again. LaWanda didn't realize how much of a lush she was. But that was her girl. Toya had been the first girl to invite her to sit with her and two of their other girlfriends. Although Toya had known the other two girls longer, she and LaWanda grew closer. What LaWanda really loved about Toya was her outgoing personality. She was always making jokes and being silly but when LaWanda wanted an honest opinion about something, she knew she could go to Toya.

"Come on, let's go wait outside. Larry should be pulling up any minute."

The evening had cooled the hot temperature of the early afternoon sun. LaWanda and Toya walked to the front of the apartments. There was a lot more traffic than usual on the street. Everyone seemed to be going out to enjoy their Friday night. Ms. Yums' blue station wagon turned into the apartment parking lot and stopped a few feet from where Toya and LaWanda stood. The rear passenger side window came down and Lucinda stuck her head out. "Where ya'll two hot tamales going?" she asked.

"Hey Cinda. Hey ya'll," Toya said speaking to Lucinda and

## Finding Daddy

giving a general wave to everyone else in the car.

"Where ya'll coming from?" LaWanda asked.

"We went to go see *Annie* the stage play. It was hype. You should've come."

"Did you take an Atlanta Braves cap out my room?"

Lucinda gave LaWanda a strange look. "Why would I do that, I don't even like the Braves and I don't wear caps."

"I just can't find it. I had it right on top of my dresser." "Well you might need to check around your room."

"Yeah, I guess it will turn up. Are you going to be at the house tonight?"

"No. I'm staying next door. Why, what's up, where ya'll headed?"

"We going to the rink."

"Ya'll better hurry up. The last bus leaves going that way at eight. It's a quarter to eight now."

Toya laughed. "The bus!" She said it like the bus was the most oddest mode of transportation she had heard of.

"Yes, the bus. How else you getting there? You ain't got no car."

Toya spun around and looked at LaWanda and began laughing.

"Naw we ain't got no car, but we definitely got a ride."

"Yeah, ride with who?" Lucinda asked looking at LaWanda suspiciously.

Before either Toya or LaWanda could respond, Larry pulled up in his brother's red Volkswagon Jetta. The passenger window came down and sitting in the passenger's seat was Jimmy from Jennings Homes. LaWanda hadn't seen him since the day he had swung on the cop in the projects and damn near started a riot. "Oh, my God!" LaWanda said in shock. "Lucinda, look! It's Jimmy from Jennings Homes."

Lucinda jumped out of the Yums' car leaving them looking after her confused as she ran around the Jetta to the passenger's side. She cupped her hand over her mouth and gasped, "Oh My God! Jimmy! What are you doing over here? Get out the car give and me a hug. This is our friend from the projects." Lucinda yelled over the car to the Yums, who were still looking on bemused by all that had happened.

Jimmy opened the car door and stepped out. He was wearing a blue Adidas tracksuit and some blue and white Adidas. His hair was cut in a neat brush cut. Waves chased the edges of his sharp line up. His trim was neat as a pin around the goatee he had grown since the last time LaWanda and Lucinda had seen him. He had gotten more muscular and taller as well. He was "5 11." His fingers donned huge gold rings and he had a big gold chain on his neck, with a big gold African charm attached to it. He stepped forward with a smile and gave Lucinda a hug. "How you been girl? How's your brother?"

"Oh my god," Lucinda said, hugging Jimmy tightly. "We been doing good, Mama still working... Henry, you know, he pulled down some time from the state," Lucinda said her voice breaking off as she spoke about her brother.

"Yeah, I heard 'bout that. What's up, Wanda?" Jimmy said stepping up to give LaWanda a hug.

"Hey, Jimmy. I ain't seen you in so long, you got so big. Looking all grown," LaWanda said, laughing and rubbing some fingers over the hairs on his chin.

Toya coughed and nudged LaWanda with an elbow. "Oh, Jimmy, this your date, my girl Toya," LaWanda said with a proud smile on her lips.

"Date!" Lucinda screamed. "Yes. Date," Toya said.

"Hey hey. Can a brother get some love?" Larry said, stepping out the vehicle.

"Aww. Come here baby," LaWanda said extending her arms. Larry embraced LaWanda. She smelled the scent of his Gucci cologne; she also smelled the scent of alcohol. "Hey, it's getting late. We gotta get going," Larry said.

"Yeah," LaWanda said, remembering they had to stop and pick up the bottle of gin from Toya's brother. "We gotta make a stop at Toya's house real quick."

"For what ?" Larry asked.

LaWanda looked at Lucinda then back at Larry. "I'll tell you on the way."

Lucinda looked on as they piled into the Jetta. "Thanks for asking if I wanted to go."

"Girl it's too late...we gotta go...we ain't got time to wait. I thought you were staying the night next door," LaWanda said,

## Finding Daddy

really ready to leave and go get the gin from Toya's brother.

"I'm just playing. I'll see ya'll later," LaWanda said, going back to get in the Yums' car.

Once everyone was in the car Larry turned on the car radio and Eric B and Rakim came through the car speakers. "So what were you going to tell me?" Larry asked.

LaWanda told Larry they needed to stop to pick up a bottle of gin from Toya's brother. That was when Jimmy pulled a bottle of Tequila from between his legs. "What do we need to go get that for. We got this."

"What is that?" Toya asked.

"This right here is top shelf baby. We drank nothing but the best." Jimmy said, giving Larry some skin, as they began laughing.

"Well, I have to go get the gin to replace the almost empty bottle at my house. Ms. Thang right here kept turning up the bottle and now my Mama's gin is almost gone."

"Oh, like I was drinking by myself," Toya remarked.

Jimmy started laughing. "Yeah, Ms. Mary don't play. You better take her to get that gin."

"Yeah, because if you don't this might be the last time we see each other, ever," LaWanda said, with a nervous laugh.

"So you use to live in the same projects?" Toya asked Jimmy. "Yeah, we use to live in the same projects before they got like the Jeffersons and moved on up."

"So you still live in the projects?"

"Yes. Ain't got no plans to move. All my peoples is right there," Jimmy turned the bottle up to his mouth and guzzled the Tequila.

"Let me taste that," Toya said, reaching to the front seat for the bottle. She took a long swig and offered the bottle to LaWanda.

"No, I'm cool. I don't want nothing else to drink and you don't need anything else either."

"Girl, I'm fine. Trust me," Toya slurred.

Toya, Larry, and Jimmy just kept passing the bottle around drinking. They were so caught up in their drinking that Larry missed the turn to Toya's street. "Hey, you missed the turn!" LaWanda screamed.

Larry swung the steering wheel hard to the left the car spun out of control in a fishtail and when Larry finally got the car under control he was back in the lane he had just turned out of, facing on coming traffic. A bright pair of headlights were coming right at them. The last thing LaWanda remembered was hearing the screeching of tires and herself scream.

When LaWanda came to, she was in a hospital bed with an I.V. in her right arm. There was a breathing apparatus attached to her nose and mouth. Her vision was still a little blurry, but her eyes were slowly starting to focus. Her body ached liked crazy and she felt a huge knot on her head. She saw Lucinda and Mary standing close to the bedside. Her uncles were gathered at the foot of her bed. Her Uncle Harvey had a smile on his face. "I knew my baby was going to be alright. You scared us there for a minute."

"Oh, thank you Jesus," Mary said. "Go get the nurse, Lucinda. Tell her your sister woke up."

Lucinda hurried from the room and returned with the nurse a few short moments later. The nurse came in the room and pressed her index and middle finger to LaWandas' wrist. "How are you feeling young lady? You gave your folks quite a scare. You're going to be fine though." The nurse pulled a pad and a pen out of her crisp white shirt and wrote down the results of LaWanda' pulse. Next the nurse removed the breathing apparatus from LaWanda's face. "Can you speak?"

LaWanda's mouth was parched and her voice was almost inaudible. It looked as if she was just moving her lips. Mary and Lucinda both leaned closer trying to hear what she was saying. Lucinda barely heard her but she understood. "What is she saying?" Mary asked.

"She's asking about Larry, Toya, and Jimmy." Lucinda said. The nurse looked at Mary and the others with questioning eyes.

Mary nodded. "Your friends were brought in with you. Toya is down the hall; she has a concussion and a broken arm, she was lucky. Larry is still in surgery; he suffered some serious injuries but he should recover. Jimmy didn't make it. He passed away in surgery about an hour ago. You are all very lucky. Everyone in that vehicle could've been killed. The driver of the other car walked away with a couple of bumps and bruises but it could've been much worse. The police are going to want to get a statement from you. They're probably going to want to know

## Finding Daddy

where you guys got the alcohol. I suggest you be honest. It will be in your best interest to cooperate. I'll have the other nurse bring you in something for the pain. I'll let the officers know you should be ready to speak with them in a few hours. Talk to your family for awhile and get some rest. I'll be back to check on you soon."

The nurse placed the breathing apparatus back in place on LaWanda's face. She nodded to the family and left the room.

LaWanda was still in pain, but now she felt sick. Jimmy had died; she couldn't believe it. She squeezed her eyes shut. The police wanted to talk to her and worst of all her Mama knew she had been drinking. She wish she could just die. Larry was in surgery. The nurse said he should recover, but it didn't matter. Mama was never going to let her see Larry again. Her life was over. Tonight was supposed to be one of the happiest nights of her life, instead it was the worse night she could ever remember. She'd never forget this night. She had three cracked ribs, a concussion, and a broken leg but her worst injury was her broken heart. And to top it all off, she never got a chance to show Courtney up.

## CHAPTER 7
### RUN DOWN ON PRISON GROUNDS

The county jail's recreation yard was a little bigger than a football field. The outer circumference of the yard was a dirt track which ran around the recreation yard. The yard was equipped with a basketball court and a weight pit. Inmates could walk the track or spend their time shooting hoops or working out. Henry had started hitting the weight pit on a regular basis. He was trying to prepare himself for state prison. He wanted to make sure he was physically fit to deal with some of the obstacles prison life was going to offer. He had heard so many stories about what goes on in the state prison system. He had heard how young men would be victimized upon reaching the state facilities. Young boys forced to be men in an environment that was controlled and destructive. A place where Mama couldn't come and pick you up when you fell down. Henry was determined to be a man. He had been doing a lot more reading lately at the suggestion of Joe. Joe had been grooming him and had become like an unofficial father figure.

Henry lay down on the weight bench and lifted the bar. He showed no signs of strain as he pressed the 225 pounds, bringing the bar down to his chest and lifting it back up. Kenny, another young boy from the projects, was spotting him as he pressed the weight.

"Come on give me one more," Kenny said, as Henry tried to place the weight bar back on the bench. He brought the weight down to his chest again and pushed it up. Just as he was guiding the bar back to the support handles which held the weights when they weren't being used, he heard voices being raised. Henry placed the bar on the bench and sat up. He looked toward the basketball court and saw some guys gathering together. "What's going on over there?" Henry asked Kenny.

"I don't know. It looks like some of the young boys 'bout to jump on old man Joe."

"Joe. Hold up," Henry said, raising up from the bench and heading toward where the crowd was gathering.

Henry brushed past a few of the boys standing surrounding Joe. He knew most of the guys standing around. Cory, a young brother from around Jennings Homes was in Joe's face. "Listen here, you hype. You owe me two packs of cigarettes. I don't care where you get them from but you better be coming up with my squares or I'm going to knock your base head out right now," Cory smirked and looked around for the support and reaction of his homeboys he had with him.

Henry was standing at the front of the crowd with his arms folded across his swollen chest. "What's going on here, Cory ?" Henry asked.

"You know Henry, just keeping these hypes in line. Joe here owe me some me from the outs. I ain't been able to catch up with him until now. So I figures he gives me two packs of cigarettes now and we call it even."

Cory had just arrived at the jail two days ago. Henry read exactly what this was. Cory was trying to shake Joe down. This wasn't about no debt from the street. Everyone in the neighborhood knew if you gave a hype something on credit, it was just like it was for free. A hype wasn't worried about paying no debt, all they wanted to do was get high. Cory had probably been booked with no money or the police had taken whatever money he had when he got booked. Either way, Henry knew Cory was trying to shake Joe down. He was trying to play on Joe to get a few packs of squares and Henry didn't like it. Joe had opened his eyes to so much in these last few months. Ever since Joe started talking to him that early morning, his thinking changed. Joe had even encouraged him to look for his biological father. He had given him all the proper information on where and how to start his search and had even written a cover letter for him. Henry was surprised at how well Joe wrote, especially knowing that he received a check every month for being legally blind. Joe explained being declared legally blind didn't mean he couldn't see, and he had surely learned to read long before he had started losing his sight.

Henry had grown a bond with Joe. He no longer looked at Joe as a hype. Joe was more like his mentor now, a shadowy father

# Finding Daddy

figure of sorts. Henry knew Cory and most of the younger brothers standing around. They were all a few years younger than him. Kenny had eased up alongside Henry. "Hey, what's up bro'?" Kenny asked.

    Henry ignored the question from Kenny. Henry looked Cory right in his eyes as he spoke. "Look here, Cory, what happened on the outside happened on the outside. We all in the same boat round here. This man in here just like you, he ain't got nothing; somebody taking care of him while he in here. I tell you what, if you want a couple cigarettes to hold you over until your peoples come and put some money on your books, I'll give you a half a pack."

    Cory looked at Henry then he looked around at the faces of his Homeboys. He started to laugh. "Man Henry, to hell with this hype, man! I want my money!"

    Henry took a few steps forward placing himself right at Cory's chest. He gazed in his eyes and did not blink. "So you don't want the half of pack?"

    Sensing the tension that was building, Cory tried to smile to relieve some of the static. "Hey Henry what's going on here? You sound like you taking up for this hype; he ain't nothing but an addict, man."

    Henry pointed his index finger in Cory's chest, "Listen here Cory, this somebody daddy you talking bout right here. What if this was your pops and some young punk was trying to shake him down?" Henry paused to let the effect of his insult sink in. He took his finger from Cory's chest and began to address the crowd standing around. "This man old enough to be your dad, man. A lot of ya'll standing here right now don't even know where your dad is at. What if ya'll pops was in here getting harassed. I ain't going for nobody picking on the weak." Henry turned back to Cory. "I'm taking over his debt, man, and I ain't got nothing for you. So, what's up?"

    Cory looked at Henry with genuine shock then he looked at Joe. "Hey, man, you best be coming to see me when you get out." Cory said, and eased through the crowd followed by a couple of his homeboys.

    "You alright old timer?" Henry asked Joe.

    "Yeah, young blood. But why you go get yourself caught

up in some mess?"

"It's no mess. Just trying to change my ways and my thinking."

"That's the first step toward being a man. You know, when I was young, I went to go stay with my uncle for awhile, me and my brothers. I swear this man worked on the railroad, hard labor, and he would come home from work dog tired, but it never failed...if my aunt came to him with a report of his sons, me or my brothers cutting up, it would seem like he got new strength to beat us. One day he took us out fishing and we out on the lake in this little boat and my uncle falls asleep, right there in the middle of the lake on the boat. We all started laughing and making jokes until my uncle woke up. Then one of his sons asked him, "Daddy how you going to bring us fishing and go to sleep?" My uncle looked at his son with a serious face, "Boy, the reason I'm out here sleep is because this is the only place I can get some proper rest. I work all day long hours in the hot sun. Then I come home and you boys got another job for me. Why you think I beat you so hard? I ain't mad at you. When ever you did what you did I was at work, but I know if I don't come home and deal with you, I'm going to have to deal with your mama, and she don't fight fair. I'll never win that fight. See, if I bring you fishing with me, I can go home and love my woman cause I know you ain't did nothing that's going to hurt us all." I strangely grasped my uncle's point that day. I see you are slowly grasping mine. Thanks, young blood."

"Hey man, don't mention it. Gotta exercise lessons learned right, otherwise they're lost." Henry turned to Kenny. "Hey man, I'm going to take a break for the rest of the day, kick it with the old timer and try and learn something."

"Okay cool bro'. I'm gonna knock out some more sets. I'll get Spider to spot me. You sure everything cool?"

"Yeah, everything is straight. I'll get up with you on the tier later." Henry gave Kenny some dap and turned back to Joe. "So let's walk, old man. Tell me some more about this uncle, he seems interesting."

"Yeah Uncle Charles was a character. Have you started looking into finding your father?"

Henry cracked a smile. "I sure did. I got a list of last known addresses. The most recent one was in Philly. I think my mother

## Finding Daddy

told me my dad had an aunt that lives there."

"So did you write to see if it's him?"

Henry looked down at his shoes and shook his head. "I don't know if it's the right address or not. What if it ain't him or it's the wrong address?"

"Do you really want to find your daddy, boy?" Joe put emphasis on the word boy. "If you really want to find him, you write all the addresses. You got nothing but time in here. You can use it wisely or you can just sit here and wait to get out with the same thought process you had when you came through these gates. These white folks don't care one way or the other. They banking on you coming back in here over and over again. They know most of us ain't smart enough to change our thinking while we in here, so we'll be back. Maybe finding your daddy will help you better understand who you are and shape you into a better man."

Henry furrowed his brow. "So you don't think I'm a man?"

See, young blood, the most important thing you can do in life is listen. I said make you a better man. You're obviously unhappy with the man you are now. Look around us." Joe waved a hand around like he was describing a beautiful landscape. "How many of these cats in here you think know exactly where their father is and can get in touch with him right now? How many of 'em do you think might not even know their father at all. I'm not talking about mommie's boyfriend or a step dad. I'm talking 'bout their dad. Most of us in here suffer from the same conditions. Just like you was telling Cory. How many of these young brothers in here you think decided on their own when they were a man, or got placed in a situation where they are forced to make grown up decisions.

Listen, young blood, you gotta realize you are at the top of the list of things that need to be destroyed. Don't be self destructive. Peer pressure and false pride is the death of man's character. How many times you see these brothers in here go to the library through the week, but every time they open up this yard there's a stream of old and young black faces running out here to kick the jive. You know my Uncle Charles used to say if you want to hide something from the black man, put it in a book. I gave you the tools to find your daddy cause you said that's what you want to do, but you won't even use 'em. You would've been better off letting Cory knock me upside the head. If you really serious about change, start doing different things. Your results will be different too."

"So you think I should try to write the old man?"

"No. I think you should do whatever you feel you need to do." Henry smiled. "The difference between a boy and a man."

"So, you have been listening when I talk. That's a start and a great quality to have. The most important thing you can do in this world is listen. If you don't know what's going on, listen. Someone will always let you know. Don't be afraid to ask, young blood."

"Let me ask you a question Joe. How did you learn how to read and write so well if you been going blind since thirteen?"

Joe laughed so hard he began to cough. "Well, young blood, I been going blind since thirteen. I ain't went blind yet. I knew early in life no one was going to be around to hold my hand. I had no choice but to catch on quick. Imagine going to school all day then coming home to Mama passed out drunk or laid up with some man, not making dinner, not helping with homework, not even worried about how your day went. When it's like that, you learn real quick ain't nobody in this world going to hold your hand and guide you through. I learned how to read and write because I knew nobody was going to do it for me. My sister Carol and me are the only two of my mama's children that can read. My brothers got to depend on everybody to do things for them. They can't even go in the supermarket with a list of grocery items. Can't sit and read with they kids, nothing. Yeah, I ain't nothing but a junkie, but that's just on the surface. Beneath the surface I am a man of learning. A wise man can play the part of a fool but a fool can never be a wise man. He is only what he is, a fool. Before we started talking you probably had me pegged as an old fool."

"I never…"

Joe cut him off. "It's cool, young blood. That's all I had shown you. I don't care what no one thinks about me. I told you foolish pride is the destruction of man. Get your pride in order. Are you capable of thinking for others?"

"Yes."

"Well, if you think you are capable of thinking for others, you should have no problem making decisions for yourself. I've made some terrible decisions in my time, but they were my decisions. Make sure you sit well with your choices. Don't make

# Finding Daddy

excuses but acknowledge the harsh realities of this world. You have to first become a man then you have to learn how to live as a black man in this white man's world. I'm not saying blame the white man for your problems, but know the way of the world and prepare yourself for it."

"So you think the white man plays no part in the destruction of the black man?"

"Never said that, young blood, but the destructive behavior of the black man assists in the process. Mostly due to lack of knowledge of the system that binds them. We'll take the time out to learn every new soul record that comes out, but how many of us know the words to the Constitution? How can you argue your rights if you don't know what they are? You think this is a coincidence that we are here? We are here by design. If you don't know or if you don't educate yourself, how can you prevent it? The same way they work to keep us at each other's throats in here is the same way they work to keep us separated on the outside long before we get here. A lot of people used to think my uncle Charles babbled when he got drunk, but a drunk man speaks a sober tongue;it's the drunk ears that misinterpret. My uncle would say things that would have me sitting around stuck for hours. One day Uncle Charles said something so profound it never left me. He said, *'We condemn our women with our destructive behavior as men, pimping them out, beating them, not being around to take care of our kids. Forcing her to take our kids and put them on the system, a system that is designed to make a nation of people complacent. Not wanting more or even willing to explore outside the invisible walls that stand around the ghetto. We are satisfied with low income housing, food stamps, and not having enough. How could the same people who worked the soil of this country for years without labor wages, become lazy and complacent when a wage is offered?'* I thought about that every day since the words left his mouth. There is no reason for us to be in the position we are in as a people. We have to change our thinking, young blood. When you write to your father, write as a man first and a son second. Maybe some of the lessons you've learned in life in his absence will make him a better man if he hasn't already become one. Remember life is a learning process, some learn quicker than others. Can you dig where I'm coming from, young blood?"

Henry nodded. His mind was going in a million different directions. He was thinking about his life, his father, Robert, his mother and his sisters. He sat in his cell that night and began writing to his dad. He wrote a long detailed letter, expressing all his feelings over the years. He talked about the lack of love he felt from Robert, his hatred for his father for leaving him. He talked about the trouble he had been into and why he felt he turned to the streets. He talked about his love for his mother and sisters and even the misplaced love he had for the man his mother said was his daddy. He ended the letter expressing his need to know who he was and where he came from. When he sealed the envelope, he felt a burden lift from his heart.

# CHAPTER 8
## NEW SCHOOL AND NEW NEIGHBOORHOOD

By the time I turned fifteen, things in my life were changing. The biggest change was the new house Mama had moved us to. It was amazing; we had our own house with a big fenced in yard. The house was in a sub-division called Butler Manor and it sat on a corner lot. The house was a four bedroom ranch-style home with a huge driveway. Mama used to close the gates to our driveway when she got in from work and they would remain closed until she was ready to go out. I remember I used to hate having to go open that gate before we pulled out. I didn't understand why she didn't just leave the gate open, it wasn't like we were still living in the projects, no one was going to steal the car or nothing. We almost got into a wreck every time we backed out our driveway. The way the house sat on the corner made the driveway a blind spot, well, our entire house really. The corner lot the house was situated on had a sharp narrow right turn. It was more like a curve in the road. We had seen so many accidents on that corner. It seemed like someone was always losing control on that turn. A few times the property owner had to come by and replace parts of the fence around the house because some driver had lost control.

I loved our new house though. Having our own yard was amazing mostly because Mama allowed us to get a puppy. My Uncle Harvey had come over with a few of his friends and painted the whole house. We got to choose what color we wanted our rooms. The house was huge, too. It had a large front porch with a rustic style cedar porch swing. I would sit on the porch at night and watch the stars. I would sometimes think about my dad. I used to wonder if he ever thought about us or if he was out there looking for us. We had moved away from the projects and that was the last time we had seen him. I loved that swing; it was so relaxing and comforting. Mama put a plush emerald green carpet down throughout the whole house except the foyer and the kitchen. We had to take our shoes off in the foyer. Mama was so serious about that carpet we couldn't even walk on it if our socks weren't clean. Our living room was decorated with leather furnishings and glass table tops and lamp stands. Mama had bought a new T.V., too, a 25 inch Zenith. The only piece of furniture in the living room from our old apartment was an old wicker chair.

    The dining room was big also. We had a huge polished oak table with six matching oak chairs. We would get some extra chairs at Thanksgiving time when my Aunt Shirley didn't host at her house. We'd sit around the table and join hands and pray before we ate. Everyone would be there: My Uncles Harvey, Clyde, Clarence, Aunt Shirley and her friend Benny, Aunt Beverly, and Nana. The only people that were missing would be Henry and my dad. I would try not to think about it but it was hard. Especially thinking about my dad and wondering if he was eating dinner with another family. I would always ask God to bring him back to us during our prayer. I would be hoping someone would ring the bell during our meal and I would go to the door and he would be there smiling holding his arms out for me. But that never happened. My Uncle Harvey would be running back and forth all day to the store for the little extras like aluminum foil and seasonings. Nana would be shouting cooking instructions to Mama and my aunts from the dining room table. Whispering to me how she knew they were in there not paying attention to her, as I sat at her side and read *Hardy Boy* mysteries to her. Nana loved *Nancy Drew*. But she couldn't read the little dime store paper backs anymore due to her eye condition. The fact is Nana had been declared legally blind long ago.

    I cherished my time with Nana, though. I had started spending a lot of time at her house. My Uncles Clarence and Clyde stayed with her but it was Uncle Harvey who did all the maintenance on the house. I spent a lot of my summer days over there. During the school year, Mama would let me go over there on the weekends. Nana always wanted me to fry pork chops; I think it was her favorite meal. She would even try to get Mama to fry some

## Finding Daddy

on Thanksgiving, but Mama refused to fry pork chops in her kitchen on Thanksgiving. Uncle Harvey would fry a turkey and everyone would be happy including Nana. The days I spent with Nana were full of tales that held the tones of antecedence. The tales she told about her grandparents and parents were so revealing to me, but I always felt like something was missing; a piece of me that her enlightening couldn't fulfill. Nana always spoke her mind. It didn't matter who she was talking to. I think Mama probably got that quality from her. She made those Thanksgiving occasions so special and memorable. By the end of the evening we'd all be gathered in the living room singing Otis Redding and Sam Cook while Nana rocked back and forth with a smile on her face.

    The day after Thanksgiving, LaWanda, Mama, and I would put up the Christmas tree. I remember us worrying about where to put the tree the first year we were in the house. The only space in the living room was in front of the fireplace that we never used because we didn't know how. Mama was scared to put the tree in front of the fireplace because of all the fires that get reported were due to Christmas trees. Mama called Uncle Harvey over and he laughed at all of us. He showed us how to work the fireplace and then he helped us put up the Christmas tree. I still remember how bright the lights were. They used to reflect off the window pane in my room at night with such luminescence, I could read the colors written on the nail polish bottles on my dresser. I painted my room a pale pink with white trim running around the boarders. Mama bought us all new furniture, too. I had a polished oak dresser with matching night stands, one placed on each side of my new queen size bed. I kept a lamp on the night stand to my left, the one closest to the window. I liked to read at night and I would have my light on late into the morning hours. I'd hear the cars outside my window braking hard as they came around the curve on Morgan Road. Early on Saturday mornings, I could hear lawn mowers humming outside. Sometimes I'd crack my window and let the smell of the fresh cut grass come through the window and fill up my room. Our dog Rusty would be running around the yard barking at the loud buzzing of the lawn mower blades. LaWanda and I were spared the task of cutting the huge lawn around the house and the yard; Uncle Harvey would come every two weeks and cut it. He did a lot of the work around the house. Mama was still working the grave yard shift and pulling down extra hours.

 LaWanda had to transfer from Hephzibah High School because it wasn't in our new school district, but she was still hanging with Toya. When she had come home from the hospital after the accident, LaWanda didn't want to go outside. She felt real bad, we all did. Especially after we went to Jimmy's funeral. Mama had even taken a day off from work to attend. We saw so many old faces from the projects. It was sad. We attended the service but we didn't go to the burial. LaWanda said her leg had started hurting and she wouldn't be able to stand with her crutches. I recall us stopping at the same McDonald's we had went to with our daddy on the way home. Toya had started driving and came to our house everyday to pick LaWanda up for work. They were working at an Albertson's supermarket across town. Mama would always caution them about driving safely before they left the house. Mama had promised to help LaWanda get her own car before graduation. I couldn't wait for LaWanda to get her car so we could go cruising. The one thing I was happy about was that we were both attending the same school again.

 LaWanda and I would hang out on Friday nights and Saturday afternoons if she wasn't working. We would go to the high school football games on Friday night and the college games on Saturday. Sometimes if Uncle Harvey wasn't busy, he'd meet us at the games and we'd tailgate with him. It was so much fun; the stadium lights, the yelling fans, the players. The atmosphere was just so stimulating. My days as a track star were behind me and I had started playing softball. I used to wonder if my athleticism and love for sports came from my dad. Sports kept me motivated, being a part of something but still being able to be competitive and achieve independent success made me feel good. This quality would assist me in many life situations as I grew into womanhood. I had started forming opinions about the things I wanted to do in life. Although I loved sports, I saw myself going into the corporate side of things. I used to dream about going to New York and working on Wall Street. I didn't fully understand what they did there back then but I knew it was important and the people dressed nice.Glen Hills high school was huge. It looked like an old castle. The huge stone structure had six entrance doors in the front,the huge timber kind with the black iron bolt locks.

# Finding Daddy

The football field and track took up most of the landscape in the back of the school and ran right into a gully of trees and thick plant life. The bleachers were spread out on both sides of the field. There was a huge concession stand that sold refreshments during the games. When you entered the school, there were huge granite staircases that led up to the classrooms and lockers. The spotted marble floors were always polished. You could hear the constant squeaking of rubber on the wax as students changed classes. The cafeteria was huge, too, and it had padded seats and the food was always hot when they served it. Going to Glen Hills also made me realize the point Mama had been trying to make to us over the years. The harder you worked, the more you accomplished and the better things got. Since we had moved from the projects things had been getting better for me. I think back to that day we left, all the drama, all the sadness I had felt; LaWanda and I not wanting to leave. I was so silly back then. Since we left the projects, my life had been exposed to all types of things I may have never thought about. I had started attending better schools and living in better places. Now we were finally living in a house.

I used to walk around our sub-division scouting the neighborhood. Our enclave was magnificent. It ran right into another neighborhood called Twin Oaks. Most of the homes were ranch style homes with fenced in yards. All the yards were well kept and the driveways were neat and clean. A few of the homes had basketball goals set up in them and kids would be playing basketball in the driveways. It was where I had first encountered Samantha. I was walking around the neighborhood on one of my regular strolls when I came upon a group of teenagers around my age playing hoops in front of a small brick house. This was a normal activity for the neighborhood on a sunny Saturday afternoon. The thing that caught my eye though was the girl with the pretty long pigtails dribbling the ball. I slowed my pace as I approached. I was enthralled by her performance. I had never seen a girl handle the ball like her, she was better than the boys. I stopped and stood watching them play from the middle of the street. The ball rolled toward me and I knelt to pick it up. When I stood up with the ball, she was right there; the girl with the pigtails and the nice handle. She was an inch or two taller than me and I was '5 9." She had a brown complexion and sharp eyebrows. Her eyes were a bright brown that seemed to match her complexion. I offered her the ball and she smiled, "Thank you. I'm Samantha," the girl said, tucking the ball beneath her left arm, and offering me her left hand.

"You're welcome. I'm Lucinda," I said, accepting her hand.

You're real good," I said pointing at the ball tucked under her arm.

"Thank you. You play?"

"No, I wish. I play softball."

"Oh, okay. Us girls gotta do something to show these boys we can hang with them on all levels."

"Come on or throw the ball back over here. You can talk to her after the game or in school."

It was Kevin who had shouted over at us. He lived a few houses down from me. I think he liked me; he always talked to me in the mornings on the bus on the way to school. "You go to Glen Hills ?" I asked.

"Yeah. I play for the girls basketball team. Who's your first period?"

"I have Ms. Malone."

"Oh, you're a sophomore. I'm a senior and the softball team doesn't use the gym much so I never see you during our practice; if you played volleyball..." Samantha smiled and shrugged her shoulders.

I laughed, "I know right. Where's your bus stop at? I've never seen you on our bus. Do you live in the neighborhood?"

"Hey Sam! Can we get the ball?" Kevin shouted coming toward us.

Samantha bounced the ball off the concrete toward Kevin. "Here, work on your jump shot?" Samantha laughed and so did a few of the other boys standing around the hoop.

"Yeah right. I scored twelve last game and had four rebounds. What your stats look like?"

"I scored fifteen and had eight rebounds. You better practice before you step to me shorty."

"Yeah, well, you know the pigskin is my game," Kevin said. We all started laughing and Kevin just waved his hand at Samantha and headed back to the hoop. I had to admit I liked the way his legs looked in his shorts. "So where do you live?" I asked

## Finding Daddy

Samantha again.

"I live on Chestnut, but I don't take the bus. I drive to school I have to. By the time I finish up with practice I only have a half an hour to get to work from the school and I work all the way down town."

I immediately decided I liked Samantha. She was into sports just like me. I couldn't believe all this time I had never thought to go to see the female basketball team play. LaWanda and I went to most of the sports events held at the school, but we hadn't been to any of the female basketball games. I promised myself I would be at her next game.

"Where do you work?"

"I work at Woolworth & Company."

"I know where that is, I go in there every time I'm downtown to get one of those flavored ice cups. They are so good."

"The Slush Puppies. Yes girl, they are so good. Next time you come in look for me I'll hook you up."

"Okay cool. I'll do that." "So where you live at?"

"I live on Morgan Road with my mother and sister LaWanda. She's a senior at Glenn Hills."

"Does she play sports, too?"

"No, but we do try to go to all the games. I'm going to try to come to your next game."

"For real? I'll be looking for you. I think we play next Friday night. It's an away game, if you can't get a ride, I'll drive you."

"I might have to take you up on that offer. My sister hasn't got her car yet; she's supposed to get it soon."

"Hey, don't worry about that. I can pick you up and we can go hang out after the game. Have you ever been to Topics?" Topics was a teen club near downtown. I had never been but I heard all about it. A lot of the kids from school went to the club on the weekends. I think LaWanda and Toya had even been to the club a few times. The D.J. spun records at the local radio station, too. I had always been curious about the club when the other kids talked about it. I was really starting to like Samantha. I had been in the neighborhood six months and this was the first time I had ran into another girl that I really considered becoming friends with.

LaWanda and I had met other girls in the neighborhood, but most of them were a little prissy. Their attitudes made them seem like they thought they were better than people. When LaWanda and I first moved around here and started hanging with the girls, they started acting differently once we told them we used to live in the projects. I didn't feel that vibe from Samantha. "No, I never been to Topics. I heard about it though. Is it nice?"

"It's alright. It's not like the teen clubs in Atlanta, but it's cool. I know all the security that be up in there. I know the guy that work the door, too, so me and my friends only pay half price. Don't worry, girl, I got you. We're going to have a good time. You should see if your sister wants to come with us."

"I will. Thanks. Did you used to live in Atlanta ?"

"Yeah we moved here from Atlanta about two years ago. My dad's job got transferred here and we had to move. I didn't like it at first but I'm getting used to it. It's a lot different from living in College Park, but hey, we're all together. At first I thought my mom and me were going to have to stay in Atlanta; she was having a lot of trouble finding a job down here. Luckily, something came through at the last minute. I don't know how things would've turned out if my mother wouldn't have found that job. I would've probably been coming down here for the summers and as often as my mother would've been driving down here; which would've probably been every weekend knowing my mom."

"You don't have any brothers and sisters ?"

"No, it's just me. You are so lucky you have a sister."

"I have a brother too. His name is Henry, he's older than me and LaWanda. He got into some trouble, but he should be home soon."

"My Uncle Dave is locked up, too. He's always getting in trouble. He'll get out for about six months and then right back in he goes. I think he likes it in there. It's just you, your sister, and mom. Does your father live near by?"

I knew she was going to ask about my dad. She seemed so proud when she spoke about her dad. I wanted so badly to make up a story about how LaWanda and I spent summers with our dad, but Samantha seemed so nice and genuine, I just couldn't bring myself to do it. "No, my dad doesn't live in Georgia. He lives in North Carolina. I really don't see him much. He's in the military. It's been

## Finding Daddy

just me, my sister, and mother for the longest. My uncle comes over and helps us out with a lot of things."

"Yeah, three women in one house. I hope ya'll got two bathrooms," Samantha said laughing.

"We do," I laughed. "It is so hot out here. I need something cold to drink."

"Let's walk to the candy lady's house. She always got some ice cold pops. She might even have some freezies."

"The candy lady. There's a candy lady around here? I've been walking all the way to the store out on the main road. I haven't been to a candy lady since we left the projects. Is it a far walk?"

"No, just around the corner. You know that big blue house that be having all the cars in the driveway ?"

"The one with the boat in the yard ?"

"Yes. That's the candy lady. Ms. Williams. She sell everything."

"Wait until I tell LaWanda. Every time we walk to the store, we be saying how we miss the candy lady."

We walked to the candy lady and bought some freezy cups. We walked around the neighborhood talking until it was almost time for her to go to work. We had so many like interests. She had been a tom boy just like me when she was younger. She lived in a nice four bedroom ranch. Her mom and dad had went away for the weekend. I waited in her room while she took a shower. Her room was nice and neat. She had a queen size bed just like mine. She also had her own stereo system and her own 19" color T.V. There were huge stuffed animals all around the room and her wall was full of posters of all types of basketball players. I walked over to her dresser to get a better look at the picture sitting on it. It was a framed photo of Samantha when she was young with a man I knew had to be her father. They had the same complexion and eye color. The woman in the photo had a light complexion and long wavy hair. She was so pretty. They were all smiling and looked so happy. I started thinking about the old photos we had at the house with daddy in them. I realized what was missing in those photos, we were never all together in those pictures like a family. There would be different shots of us, maybe LaWanda and I with daddy, or Mama and daddy together; but never all of us as a family.

"I see you met my folks. I was ten in that picture," Samantha said, grabbing her car keys. "You ready? I'll drop you off at home."

"Okay, thanks."

Samantha drove a pea green '78 Mustang. It was a nice little car. We got in the car and she fired up the engine. The first thing I noticed was that the car was a stick shift.

"You know how to drive a stick shift?"

Samantha laughed. "If I don't, nobody has noticed yet. It's easy. . I've been driving since I was twelve. I learned how to drive with a stick shift. My dad had a stick shift. Soon as I could reach the pedals and look over the dash he began teaching me to drive. I'll teach you how to drive a stick one day, it's easy," she repeated.

"Are you serious?"

"About teaching you to drive a stick or me driving since I was twelve?"

"Both," I laughed.

"Yes, to both," Samantha laughed.

She expertly slipped the car in gear and we were off. She drove me to my house breaking way before she got to the curve, where so many other cars lost control. "You don't know how many times someone has almost hit me coming round that curve. Somebody is really going to get hurt bad one day if they don't fix this street."

"I know. Sometimes I think someone is going to bust right through the fence and run right into our house. Thank you, Samantha," I said getting out the car.

"Your welcome and Lucinda?"

"Yes?"

"Call me Sam please."

"Alright. Thank you, Sam."

"Now, didn't that feel much better?" Sam said laughing. "Don't forget to call me. I'm off tomorrow."

"I will. Be safe."

"You too. Later."

I looked after her car after she had pulled off. She was cool. I was looking forward to hanging out with her. That day was the beginning of one of the most meaningful friendships I would have.

# CHAPTER 9
## CLUB TOPICS: THE HOT SPOT

The gymnasium lights were bright and the bleacher seats were filled to capacity. The cheer leading squad stomped to a rhythm that seemed to vibrate the gymnasium floor. The spectators' screams and cheers did nothing to block out the constant squeaking of athletic shoes on the gym floor. The girls on the court shouted to one another as they moved the ball around to each other in a series of passes trying to prevent their defenders from getting the ball. It was crunch time, the home team was down by one and there was only twenty-four seconds left. Sam was wearing number twenty- three. The front of the gray and black jersey she wore was sweat soaked. She guarded the girl dribbling the ball with a look of serious concentration. The girl eyed Samantha as she dribbled the ball looking for an open teammate to pass the ball to. Samantha's defense had her trapped on the outside perimeter. As soon as the girl picked up her dribble and stopped to survey the court, Samantha converged on her waving her arms as a distraction to the girl's view. The strategy worked perfectly. Just as the girl went to pass the ball to one of her teammates, Samantha reached out and deflected the ball in the other direction and gave pursuit. Samantha chased the ball down and made a fast break toward the opposite goal. The girl she had been defending was right on her heels as she ran toward the goal. Samantha laid the ball up easily off the backboard and it dropped through the net. The visiting team called a timeout and ran off to the sidelines. Samantha stood in the huddle with her teammates and listened to the coach. "Listen, their best shooter is number twelve. Sam, you been shutting her down most of the night, I need you here. They're getting the ball at half court. They'll probably inbound the ball to her. Sam, I want you all over her. They only got seven seconds to get a shot off. Don't foul! Panthers on three. One, two, three..."

"PANTHERS!"

The girls took the court and the referee gave the ball to the visiting team to inbound the ball and blew the whistle. Samantha chased number twelve around the court as the girl tried to get open for the inbound pass. The girl inbounding the ball recognized the tight defense Samantha had on her teammate and was forced to pass the ball to another player that was near by. As soon as the girl caught the pass, she tried to take a quick jumper. Soon as the ball left her hands on the way to the goal, Samantha's hand swatted it in the other direction from the goal. The ball bounced out of bounds just as the buzzer sounded calling an end to the game. Samantha's teammates ran to her excitedly and begin to hug her and jump up and down around her. Spectators started running off the bleachers to join in the celebration on the court. The gymnasium floor was packed with people. The scene looked like an NBA finals game. Samantha was all smiles in the center of the celebration. Not only had she made the winning play, she had scored twenty of her team's sixty-seven points. She had pulled down ten rebounds and five block shots. It was her best game all season. This win put them in the play-offs for the state championship.

Samantha finally broke away from the crowd and made it over to where I was standing with LaWanda and Toya. She sprinted over out of breath. "Hey ya'll, did ya'll see that block ?!" Samantha said, excited and out of breath.

"Yes girl, that was hype," I said. "Thanks! Are we still on for tonight?"

"Topics, yes," I said.

"Okay. Let me just grab my stuff. I'm going to take my shower at my house. I don't like using the school showers. You going to come to my house with me? You can meet my parents."

"Okay cool. Toya and Wanda can go to our house and get ready. a snack box or something. I haven't eaten since lunch earlier. I'm starving," Toya said patting her stomach.

"Alright. We'll meet you over at Lucinda's around nine-thirty. We should get to Topics around ten-thirty."

"Hey, ya'll. Nice game Sam," Kevin said, as he approached. Thanks, Kev. What you doing tonight?"

"A few of us were talking about going to Topics. What ya'll doing?"

# Finding Daddy

"Going to Topics. You should come. Lucinda's going to be there," Sam said, in a teasing tone.

I nudged her with an elbow. We had been talking about Kevin and my suspicions of his crush on me. Under mild interrogation, I admitted I had a crush on him, too. Ever since that little admission, Sam had been trying to play match maker. Telling me little things Kevin had told her about me and there was no doubt in my mind she was telling him the things I had said. I know because he started sitting next to me on the bus on the way to school and on the way home. Plus our conversations had changed. He now talked to me about things like what type of boys I liked and if I liked anybody at school. I answered these questions with responses that really gave away no detail at all like: "I like boys with gentlemen- like qualities because I am a lady and wanted to be treated as such." A lesson I had picked up from Nana; or "I don't really think about boys enough to like anybody because I was into my studies." I think Kevin knew I was playing hard to get because he was so persistent with his questioning. No matter how many times I gave him those answers, he kept asking the same things, sometimes more than once a day. I wanted to tell him so bad that I thought he was cute, but I was nervous.

"Oh, yeah? You going to come out tonight and party. I hope you don't start acting like you don't know me," Kevin said, with a smile.

"Yeah, I'm going to be there tonight. Why would I act like I don't know you? You live right down the street," I giggled.

Very funny. You know what I'm talking about. You know I might want to dance or something with you." "You dance?"

"Do I dance? I'm the best dancer you ever saw." Kevin moved close to Lucinda and demonstrated a few dance moves to emphasize his statement.

"Boy, you crazy," I said, pushing him softly in his chest with a palm. I felt his muscular physique beneath his shirt and felt my cheeks burn.

"Um, looks like somebody got a boyfriend," Toya teased.

"I know, right? I didn't even know about this and we all ride the bus together. So how long this been going on?" LaWanda asked.

"Ain't nothing going on!" I said, feeling my palms

~ 99 ~

beginning to sweat.

"Alright Kev, she don't want us to know. Tell us what's going on," Sam said, with a crooked smile on her face.

"Ain't nothing going on...except that Lucinda likes me and keeps trying to act like she don't," Kevin said, looking me right in the eyes.

I couldn't believe he had just said that. How could he put me on the spot like that in front of my sister and my friends? I felt embarrassed and flustered. I couldn't muster a response. Kevin had caught me so off guard with his statement. He'd never said anything like that to me before. I was ready to leave and fast. I just needed to get out the gym and into the parking lot; it felt like the walls were closing in on me. I no longer heard the cheering and celebrating of the crowd. All I heard was Kevin's words and I didn't know what to think. I just wanted to get away.

I rolled my eyes at Kevin and turned to Sam. "I'll be waiting for you outside," I said before heading toward the exit.

LaWanda and Toya caught up with me just as I stepped out into the night air. The air was cool and crisp and felt refreshing to me. I took in a deep breath, closed my eyes and exhaled. "What was that about?" LaWanda asked.

"I don't know. You know Kevin and I aren't going out."
"But you do like him, don't you?"
"I thought I did, but now I don't know. He just tried to put me on the spot."

"He didn't put you on the spot. He was just letting you know that he knew you liked him and he liked you, too, and it was alright," Toya said.

"I like Kevin. I think ya'll would be cute together," LaWanda said.

"Yeah, he's cute. I think you should go for it, girl," Toya said. "Go for what? It's not like he gave me a note with boxes saying check yes or no. He didn't ask me out."

"Girl, you are so green. That boy got the biggest crush on you. You better make your move before somebody else make theirs and you be left out in the cold."

"Well, I guess it wasn't meant to be if that happens." "Just talk to the boy tonight. It can't hurt."

"Now wait a minute, Wanda, I don't know if I agree with

you .It's going to be a lot of cuties up in there tonight and she might want to keep her options open for one more night. If guys see her stuck to one guy, she won't get no play and you know we going to be the flyest girls up in there." Toya said, looking mischievous as she smirked.

"Girl, you are crazy. We about to go, Cinda, so we can stop and get something to eat? You alright?" LaWanda asked.

"Yes, I'm fine. Sam will be out in a minute." "Alright, see you when you get to the house." " Alright, ya'll. Be safe."

I watched Wanda and Toya walk through the parking lot stopping every few steps to speak to people that were standing around cars. It usually took the school parking lot about an hour and a half to clear out after games. Security would usually have to come through and start directing people out of the parking lot. Sam finally exited the school with a few of her teammates. She stopped where I stood. "You ready?"

"Yes. I've been waiting on you." "Okay, I'm ready."

Sam said goodbye to her teammates and we made our way to her car. We climbed into the Mustang and Sam turned to me. "What's up with you and Kev?"

"Nothing. You know you the cause of all that happened tonight. If you wouldn't have been going back and forth telling him the things I've been saying, this would've never have happened."

"What I do?" Sam asked with a smile on her face.

"You know what you did. Kevin would've never said anything like that if you wouldn't have been telling him stuff."

"Somebody had to say something. Ya'll was stuck on the crush. Why are you upset? He made it known that he liked you."

"Everybody keep saying that, but all it looks like is he just made it known that I liked him. He never said anything about feeling the same way. He just made it known how I feel about him."

"That's what you want, girl. If he didn't feel the same way, he wouldn' t have said nothing. Trust me, girl, I know how these boys think. I deal with enough of them to know, trust me."

"So who do you like?" I asked.

"I like Derrick," Sam said without hesitation.

"Derrick! Not Derrick the point guard for the boys basketball team?"

"Yeah, girl. You don't see how sexy his walk is and how he dribbles the ball up the court? My dad said you can tell a lot about a player by the way they handled the ball and Derrick got handle."

"So why didn't you tell him?"

"I was trying to but I wasn't aggressive enough and he started dating Sheila McKinnley."

"So you just going to let her have your man?" I asked.

"No. I'm just letting her borrow him for awhile then I'm going to claim my prize. I let him slip away into the hands of the competition. I just don't want you to make the same mistake I made."

"I ain't going to make no mistake. If he don't ask me properly, I ain't giving him a chance to be my boyfriend. It will be his loss." "Okay. I think it's just fair to warn you that Christina Williams is digging him, too. I don't want you to be standing on the outside wondering what happened."

"I won't, trust me." I felt sure and confident about my statement, but there was something in the back of my mind tugging at me, telling me to listen to Sam. I couldn't break after what Kevin had just did. I didn't care how my sister, Toya, or Sam felt. I felt like he should've told me he liked me outright instead of the little display he made in front of my sister and friends. I might just ignore him tonight if he showed up at Topics and tried to talk to me. I didn't know how to react. This was the first time a boy had ever made me feel uncomfortable. I started thinking about my father. I wish I could talk to him. This is one of the times I needed him for guidance. I wish he was here to tell me what to do or scare the boy off because I was so scared and nervous. A part of me wanted to talk to Kevin tonight to really let him know how I felt, and another part of me wanted to just ignore him and the feelings I was having inside. I didn't know what to say to him. I hoped he didn't show up tonight. I was really thinking about just staying home. Sam must have sensed something was wrong with me because we rode in silence.

When we pulled up to Sam's house, her mother's blue BMW was sitting in the driveway. We got out the car and I walked to the BMW. "I love your mom's car. I would look so fly in this."

"You might get your wish, fly girl. She might let me use it tonight to go to the club."

## Finding Daddy

"For real? If we pull up in that, we will be the flyest chicks there," I said, forgetting all about not wanting to see Kevin at the club.

"We going to be the flyest chicks there anyway," Sam laughed. "I know, right," I said, laughing and giving her a high five. When we walked in the house, Sam's mother was in the kitchen making a salad. Sam's mom, Mrs. Jones, was so beautiful. She had long wavy hair, her skin was so light she almost looked white. Her Creole roots were barely present in her speech when she spoke and her smile was warm and welcoming. She was so cool, too. She had taken Sam and me to the mall last Sunday and got our nails and feet done. Then we went for ice cream. It was so cool. I wished I had the type of relationship Sam had with her mom. Mama was always working and even when she wasn't, we rarely shared those mother-daughter bonding moments. I knew Mama loved us, but she loved us without a show of a lot of affection. I think Mama was trying to make us tough for the world. Sometimes I wondered if our daddy left because of the way Mama loved him. Mama never talked about daddy. Every time I would bring him up she would just dismiss the subject as if I had never said anything at all. LaWanda had started feeling like Mama, too. All she looked forward to was the support checks that came for us. Was I the only one left who loved my daddy? I walked into the kitchen and gave Sam's mom a hug. "Hey, Ms. Gloria."

"Hello. How are you Lucinda?" Ms. Gloria asked, embracing me back.

"I'm alright."

"No she's not, Ma, she love sick," Sam teased.

"Love sick?" Ms. Gloria repeated looking at me with a curious smile.

"No, I'm not."

"Yes she is, Ma and guess who it is? Kevin."

"The young boy you be playing ball with sometimes?" "Yep."

"I am not!" I said trying to convince Ms. Gloria with a straight face.

"He's cute. How was the game tonight?" Ms. Gloria asked Sam.

"It was a good one. We pulled it out with only seconds left

on the play clock. Those girls were good, but you know I'm the best." Sam said laughing.

"Yes you are," Ms. Gloria agreed. "How many points did you have?"

"Twenty points, ten rebounds and five blocks." "Yeah, her last block shot won the game," I said.

"Yeah Ma, I sent that ball into the bleachers. You should've seen it."

"I wanted to be there but I had to take your father to the airport."

"I know. Is dad going to stop in Philly and see grandma?"

He said he wanted to but he didn't know if he was going to have time. He has to try and close that account deal before the weekend is out and you know these investors will try to drain you for everything they can get for free before they invest. He might spend all weekend having lunches and playing golf. Poor soul," Ms. Gloria laughed and Sam joined her.

As I watched Sam and her mother, I felt a little empty and lonely. I wished Mama and I had a relationship like theirs. Sam had a good relationship with her father, too. Last Sunday after we returned from the mall, Sam, Mr. Calvin, and I had watched a football game together. Sam and Mr. Calvin discussed the plays and joked about the commercials in between the game. I started wondering if my dad would've done that with us if he was still living with us. I never really understood why dad and Mama separated. No one ever talked about a reason. I heard Nana talk about other women, but Henry had said it was because Mama got fed up with daddy treating him differently because he was not his son. I didn't know what to think. I just knew a part of me felt empty inside and I knew it was because my daddy wasn't there. Watching Sam and her dad really touched me. I had to go in the bathroom because I felt tears swelling up in my eyes. I let the toilet cover down over the seat and sat there and cried for ten minutes. When I came back in the living room, Sam and her dad had a big bowl of nachos and a big bowl of chili sitting between them on the floor. "Hey Lucinda, come have some chili and nachos," Mr. Calvin offered.

"Yeah, girl, you gotta have some of this chili. My dad made it. It is so good."

# Finding Daddy

I joined them and we shared the nachos and chili, joked, and laughed. It felt like family. Everything was so genuine. It was amazing to me; I had just met Sam the day before. That night when I went home, I got on my knees and prayed to God that he would send my daddy back and we would have the same type of loving relationship Sam had with her dad. I was again praying, as I watched Sam and her mother.

"Hey Cinda, I'm going to go jump in the shower and get ready. Make yourself at home." Sam said, heading off to her room.

"Okay."

"Would you like some salad Lucinda?" Ms. Gloria asked.

"Sure."

Ms. Gloria took another glass bowl from the cabinet and began putting salad in it. "I added some bacon bits. Is that okay? She asked.

"Yes fine."

"I just asked because everyone doesn't eat pork. Calvin has a cousin that doesn't eat pork. He drives me nuts every time he comes to visit. Always talking about how pork is the number one killer. I just laugh at him. He talking about pork is the number one killer; he need to be worried about the two packs of cigarettes he smoke a day. I told him he keep smoking the way he do I'll bet he won't have to worry about no pork. Here you go, baby," Ms. Gloria said, handing me the bowl of salad.

"Thank you." The salad looked delectable. It had lettuce, tomatoes, red onions, shredded cheese, cucumbers, shredded carrots, and bacon bits.

"What kind of dressing do you want, Ranch or Italian?"

Italian, please."

"I like Italian, too. Is your sister going out with you guys tonight?"

"Yes ma'am. We are meeting her and our other friend Toya at my house."

"I have to meet your sister. You have to bring her over one day. Maybe Sunday I might put some meat on the grill. You can invite your mother, too. It would be nice just the girls. Calvin will be out of town until Monday."

"Okay. I'm sure LaWanda would like to come over. Mama may be working, though."

"That's fine. I would love to meet your sister. She's graduating this year, too, isn't she?"

"Yes."

"That's good. Does she have any plans for college?"

"I don't think so. She says she's tired of school. I think she's going to just work her job for awhile and see what she wants to do."

"Oh, okay. A lot of kids work for a year or so before they go to college. Where does she work?"

"She works at Albertson's."

"What about you, have you thought about what you want to do after school?"

"Not really. I still got another two years. I love sports, but I know it's hard to get a scholarship for sports. I like animals. I was thinking about going to school to be a veterinarian, but I'm really not sure."

"I know you have two years left before you graduate, but you need to start thinking about what you're going to do. There are so many choices out there for young people about to enter into that next stage in life. Sam's going to school for accounting; she wants to follow in her father's footsteps. I wanted to be a lawyer all through junior high school. By the time I graduated I had my mind set on business management."

"What happened?"

"I got a bachelors in business. I still think about what it would've been like to be a lawyer sometimes, but I have no regrets. I love my career and my family. Sometimes you have to do things in life that compliment who you are. Use your spare time to get to know yourself and the things in life that make you happy for a greater good. One day you'll have a family and you'll have to make some hard decisions. Life can throw you a curve ball at anytime."

"You sound just like my mom when you talk like that."

"Your mom must be a strong woman."

"She is," I said proudly.

"That's good. We all need that strong personality in our lives and it's grand when it's a parent or loved one that instills that in us. Peers can be so misleading."

"You and Mr. Calvin seem so happy."

"We are, but this picture is pretty because we made it like

# Finding Daddy

this. We've had our share of trials and tribulations, but at the end of the day our dedication and love for each other placed us in a peaceful place. I know you said your father doesn't live with you. Do you speak with him often?"

"No," I said in a low voice.

Ms. Gloria pursed her lips. You miss him don't you?"

"Yes."

"When's the last time you saw or heard from him?"

"It's been a long time. All we get are the support checks he sends."

"Have you tried to contact him?"

"I don't know where he is. All I know is that he's in North Carolina somewhere."

I broke down and told her all about the first time I met him in court and the second time when he came to court and the judge told him LaWanda and I were his daughters. I remembered that day so vividly as I told her about our trip to McDonald's. I told her how he had promised to come back and see us; then he left and we haven't seen him again since. We just received the checks. No birthday cards, no pictures, no letters, no phone calls. By the time I was done speaking, our salad bowls were empty and she was embracing me as my tears stained her bosom. I felt so much love in her arms in the midst of my pain. I wish mama held me like this.

"It will be alright, baby. You can't let that get you down in life. It takes a certain type of man to be a father. Maybe he was neglected as a child and is struggling with his own demons. A lot of men grow up without a father in their lives and that could affect the way they grow. I think the transition from boyhood to manhood is a very difficult step when you don't have the proper guidance."

"Hey ya'll, how do I look?"

Sam walked in the living room causing that moment I was feeling to be lost. I tucked my head as Ms. Gloria released me from her embrace. "You look great, baby." Ms. Gloria said, walking toward Sam and blocking her view to me. I took that moment to get myself together.

"Thanks Ma. What's going on in here?" Sam asked looking around her mom at me suspiciously.

"Nothing. We were just having a heart to heart. You know how emotional us women can get sometimes," Ms. Gloria turned to me and winked. "She's fine. You gotta get her to her house so she can get dolled up like you."

Ms. Gloria made me feel so good. I wasn't thinking about Kevin anymore. I just wanted to go out and have a nice time. Ms. Gloria was right about something else, too. Sam did look great. She was wearing a silver body dress and some silver open toe heels. I was in awe as I looked at her. I had never seen Sam in a dress before, she often wore sweats or jeans. The heels made her tower over me and Ms. Gloria, but she looked marvelous. Her legs were smooth and moist looking and her long hair hung below her shoulders. She walked in the heels like a professional. She walked to the middle of the room and did a full spin and held her arms out away from her body. It occurred to me for the first time how beautiful Sam really was. She had all the makings of a model: good skin, great height, and angelic features. "You're beautiful," I said.

"Girl, stop it."

"No I'm serious. You should dress like this all the time."
"And risk my starting spot on the team? No thanks."

"My angel is always trying to be the jock. If you promise not to take the tennis shoes out the house with you tonight, I'll let you drive the BMW."

"Mama, you know I can't wear no Nikes with this dress. Now let me get the keys," Sam said laughing.

Ms. Gloria smiled and headed to her bedroom to get the keys. Soon as she was out of earshot Sam turned to me and smiled. "I told you girl, we are going to be the freshest girls up in there tonight. I can't wait to pull up in front of Topics without my mother dropping me off. I bet Stanley won't be able to keep his eyes off me."

"Stan. I know you are not talking about Stan the quarterback?" "Do you know another one?" Sam said with a smile.

"You are so sneaky, girl. So that's why you been trying to get me to come watch the football team practice?"

"What?" Sam said laughing.

"And you teasing me about Kevin and you got a crush on Stan." "No I don't. He told his friend he wanted to get with me a month ago. I just been playing hard to get. I gotta teach you that, girl."

"So are you going to get with him?"

## Finding Daddy

"Of course I am. I just want him to sweat a bit."

"Well you might miss out, so many girls at school want to be his girlfriend. You better stop playing."

"Girl I ain't worried about those other girls. They want him and he wants me. Just like Kevin wants you. See, when they want us, we are in control. Never give up your control. The minute you do that, you stop becoming a lady."

Ms. Gloria returned to the living room jingling the keys to her car. She extended her arm out toward Sam and then pulled it back quickly as Sam reached for the keys. "I want you to be very careful. Safety first, fun second right?"

"Yes, mother," Sam said.

"Lucinda, keep an eye on her. She forgets sometimes she's a high school superstar. So many things can taint her image. Ya'll have a good time tonight and Sam make sure you put some gas in my car before you pull back in this driveway."

"I will, Ma."

"Goodnight Ms. Gloria," I said and gave her a big hug.

"Okay, ma. I will see you in the morning. If daddy calls tells him I love him."

"I will baby."

We got in the BMW and backed out of the driveway. Soon as we turned the corner, Sam let down the windows and turned on the radio. Special Ed's, "I Got It Made" filled the interior of the car and echoed off the homes we drove past. The leather seats felt so good. The wind blew against my face and the butterflies released from my stomach. I felt free.

"You like this song?" I shouted over the car's stereo system at Sam. "Huh?" Sam said, gripping the steering wheel with one hand and cupping her right hand to her ear with a smirk on her face. "Yeah girl, this song is dope." Sam turned the dial and the car's speakers bumped louder.

"Do you think I should put on some lipstick?" I asked Sam, noticing the fresh raspberry coat on her lips. She looked so different. She looked mature. I realized at that moment how much older than me she really was. She was graduating this year with LaWanda; she was a senior. That said something about my maturity level in her eyes. Since we had met last Saturday, we had been glued at the hip. We met each other in between periods and she started dropping by my house when her work schedule permitted it; she even said she was going to try and get me a job at Woolworth's. She was really my friend.

"Girl, what you over there thinking about so hard? I hope you ain't sweating Kevin. That boy want you. I gotta loosen you up." Sam eased off the accelerator and popped open her silver clutch bag and began sifting through the purse. She came out of the clutch with a fat joint and ran the marijuana stick under her nose. "Find that lighter in my bag," Sam said, looking at me with that smirk.

"Girl, is you crazy... is that real?"

"Forget my purse, girl." Sam pushed the lighter in next to the car's stereo.

I couldn't believe Sam was really about to smoke a joint. I would've never thought she smoked, and in her mother's car! The minute she put the lighter to the joint's tip, I got panicky. I smelled the loud odor of the marijuana as it filled the car. I started thinking we were going to go to jail. I froze up when she tried to pass it to me.

"Girl, here take a hit. You will feel so good. You'll have it made."

Was this it? Was these the times Mama had been trying to prepare me for all my life? Was this peer pressure? I obviously didn't think so because I reached out and grabbed that joint. I had no idea what I was doing, but I felt safe because I was with a friend. I put the joint to my lips like I had seen the older boys in the projects do when I was small. I sucked on the end and I saw the tip glow a fiery red as the smoke traveled to my lungs. When I exhaled, a cloud of smoke blew out the window in a long, winding stream. At the same time my chest expanded like it was going to explode and I began to cough uncontrollably. Sam started laughing and pulled the car over and turned down the radio, "Girl you alright? Open the door and get some air. Please don't throw up in here," Sam said, laughing.

I swung open my door and hung halfway out the car. I dropped the joint near the curb. I couldn't stop coughing. Sam got out the car and came around to the passenger's side. She patted me on my back while laughing. I finally caught my breath enough to speak but my mouth was dry. I took in another deep breath. "I

## Finding Daddy

gotta... get something to drink."

"Okay, we right around the corner from your house."

I began to focus and realized we were three houses away from Kevin's. I quickly pulled myself together and sat upright in the seat and closed the car door. Apparently Sam had picked up the joint when she came around the car to pat me on the back. She took another long pull on the joint and dropped it in the ashtray. "You sure you alright?" Sam asked, slipping the car back into gear and pulling away from the curb.

I was pulling myself together as best I could; my eyes felt puffy and my mouth was dry. I glanced at my reflection in the side view mirror. I looked fine aside from the fact that my eyes had shrunk to the point that I looked like I was Asian. I thought about the Yums and laughed aloud. I was feeling silly and carefree.

"Yeah, I'm good, girl. I just need something to drink." Sam hit the brakes at the curve near our driveway. She eased the BMW around the curb and pulled into our lot behind Toya's Honda Prelude. The night air felt so warm and refreshing on my face when I stepped out the car. I walked up on the porch and fumbled for my keys in my purse. "I love this swing," Sam said going to sit on the porch swing.

I finally found my keys and unlocked the front door. "Come on, girl. I gotta get something to drink and get ready."

"Yeah, it's quarter after nine already," Sam said, easing off the swing and following me into the house. I walked right past LaWanda and Toya in the living room and headed straight to the kitchen. I poured myself a large glass of apple juice and drank it down. I refilled the glass and drank it halfway down. I set the glass on the counter and headed back toward the living room. Toya and LaWanda were gathered around Sam praising her on her attire. LaWanda turned to me with a smile, "You high ain't you?"

"Wha...what, no!"

"Yeah right. Sam told us ya'll was hitting the budda" Toya said, laughing.

I looked at Sam and she had that silly smirk on her face. I felt my nerves running through my veins. Was LaWanda going to tell Mama? We never told Mama what each other did, but this was different. This was drugs. Why had Sam told them what we were doing? "I really didn't smoke it, I just put it to my lips."

"Yeah right, you can barely open your eyes, and they're all red," LaWanda said. She had a silly smirk on her face, too.

"Ya'll should've saved us some," LaWanda said, breaking into a laugh.

"We did," Sam said. "Well light it up, girl."

Was I hearing them right? I must be high. Did LaWanda say she wanted to smoke? Sam started heading toward the front door. "Where you going?" I called after Sam.

"I'm going to the car to get the joint."

"Oh no, we can't smoke in here. Mama will kill us."

LaWanda nodded her head agreeing with me. "Yeah, she's right. Let's go out on the porch. The night air will take the smell away. By the time Mama get here in the morning the smell will be gone."

For some reason I didn't think this was LaWanda's first time smoking. I didn't think she would ever drink or smoke after the car accident. Mama had lectured us for weeks; she had even poured a half gallon of gin down the toilet to try and prove to us that she was serious about us not drinking and doing drugs. We found a gallon of gin under her bed a few days later though. I guess she was just trying to teach us a lesson. Apparently it hadn't worked. "Ya'll go ahead. I'm straight. I'm going to take my shower and get ready."

"Yeah girl, hit the shower and try and pull yourself together. I got you when you get out," Sam said, with a wink.

I watched them go out the door and I headed to my bedroom to get my things ready for my shower. When I stepped under the shower head, the hot water felt so good on my skin. I just stood there until I heard someone knocking on the door. "Girl, hurry up! We gotta go!" I couldn't make out whose voice it was because the water was beating down on me.

"Here I come!" I screamed, as I began to wash myself. When I got out the shower, I slipped back in my room and began to get dressed. I was wearing a black spandex catsuit. I had planned on wearing my black mules, but after seeing the heels Sam stepped out with, I had slipped into Mama's room before my shower and gotten her black open toe heeled sandals. I stepped out of my room into blackness. The whole house was bathed in darkness. I paused before I turned out my bedroom light and stepped out into the hallway. I heard Wanda, Sam, and Toya out on the front porch.

## Finding Daddy

When I walked out to the porch they were all standing around holding green bottles and laughing. "What's wrong with ya'll and what's that ya'll drinking?"

"Private Stock, ice cold from the cooler in my trunk," Toya said.

I couldn't believe it! Wanda and Toya were drinking again after what had happened and Toya had the beer in a cooler in the trunk of her car! What if they got pulled over? Just as I was about to say something about it, Sam appeared at my side and passed me the joint. I just looked at her for a moment then I took a pull on the joint. This time, I inhaled slowly and let the smoke form at the back of my throat slowly. I felt the pressure in my chest building as the smoke made its way to my lungs; I exhaled and tried to stifle a cough. I couldn't stop it but I didn't go into the uncontrollable cough I had before. I started experiencing that magical, nonchalant feeling again. I passed the joint to LaWanda, who was looking at me smiling. She pulled on the end of the joint hard and exhaled without coughing. I was surprised at how expertly LaWanda had hit the joint; it was clear to me this wasn't her first time smoking. "It's getting late. We need to get going," I said.

"Yeah, I can't wait to get out at the club in that!" Toya said, pointing at the BMW.

"We decided it would be better to just take one car since we are all together," Sam said, moving off the porch toward the car. We all followed with me leading the pack, making sure I got the front seat.

We pulled out of our driveway and Sam turned up the radio. We all rolled our windows down and sang along with the music on the radio at the top of our lungs. Topics sat inside of a strip mall with a supermarket, a department store, a shoe store, a McDonald's, and a drug store. The only business that was still open at this hour of the night was the supermarket. Sam pulled into the Sunco gas station next to the strip mall. "Let's get some gum," Sam said, getting out of the car.

We all jumped out of the BMW strutting like superstars and looking around to see who was watching us. It may have been the joint we smoked earlier, but I felt like I was floating. Everything seemed to be moving in slow motion. I saw Kevin standing near the entrance to the gas station with his friends. Kevin eased away from his friends and approached us. "Hey ya'll, what's going on? I see your moms let you hold the car tonight" Kevin said, as he reached us.

"Hey Kev. What ya'll doing hanging out at the gas station?" Sam asked.

"We just waiting to see who coming through before we go up in the spot. What ya'll doing over here looking all good. How you doing Lucinda?"

"I'm fine," I said, making sure to maintain eye contact with Kevin.

"Yes you are fine, very fine."

I almost smiled when Kevin said that, but I remembered what Sam had said earlier about control. I kept a straight face. "I'm glad you noticed, now don't lose focus." I couldn't believe I had just said that. It must have been the weed talking, but it felt good.

Before Kevin could respond, a loud group of girls came out of the gas station. It was some girls from our school that I had a little rivalry with. Rene Coleman and her little crew. Rene played on the softball team with me but we were definitely not on the same team in life. I think she and a few of the other girls on the team were jealous of me. I had come on the team and impressed the coach so much in my first three games she made me a co-captain of the team. I guess Rene felt like I took her spot. "Hey ya'll look, it's the captain of our softball team. Where's your cleats, sweetie ?" Rene said, as she got near where we were standing.

I didn't plan to respond. I was feeling too good and I had finally turned the tables on Kevin. But then Rene and her group stopped. "Kevin I hope you ain't over here talking to this tomboy" Rene said, pointing at me.

"What?!" Sam said, stepping up close to my left side, LaWanda was already crowding my right.

I really wasn't in the mood to get in no fight tonight. I had on Mama's heels, plus I was looking too good to be out here rolling around with these girls. Then I heard a voice I hadn't heard in a longtime. "Well if it ain't Ms. Love Me in a Special Way." I was certain it was her, Sharmaine Johnson.

Who else in the gas station parking lot would remember the song I performed in junior high school. Then I saw her as she stepped from behind Rene. She was still pretty, truth is she didn't look much different since the last time I had seen her. "You know her, cuz?" Rene asked Sharmaine.

"Sure do. I used to go to school with her," Sharmaine said stepping closer to me. "Look at her now out here looking all grown up, she even got on lipstick." With that she reached out and touched her index finger to my lips and smeared my lipstick. That was all it took. I grabbed a handful of her hair and gripped it in a fist. I pulled her toward me and raked her face with the nails of my right hand. I heard her scream and she grabbed my hand that was holding her hair trying to break my grip. Then I felt one of her nails on my cheek. I let her hair go and swung a wild hay maker that knocked her off her feet. I kicked her in the stomach and began beating her head and face with my fist. Out of my peripheral, I saw LaWanda, Sam, and Toya fighting Rene and the other girls. I don't know if it was the alcohol, but I felt hype. LaWanda, Toya, Sam, and me turned that gas station parking lot out. By the time the police got there to break it up, there were at least three other groups fighting as well. It was like the whole Topics had heard about the fight and ran out the club to the gas station. It was crazy! The police had to call for back up and it took an hour before we could get in the BMW and drive out of the lot, it was so crowded. When we finally made it out of the gas station parking lot, we were moving at a snail's pace driving down the street. There were crowds of people still gathered around; police were trying to get people to move on but most of the teenagers were still being loud and unruly.

When we finally made it off the strip, I was so relieved. I kept thinking we were going to be pulled over and arrested for the fight. I felt a sting on my left cheek and touched a finger to my face, I felt a small scratch and there was a speck of blood on my finger.

We were all riding in silence and watching the street. I felt my bare feet on the floor of the car. Somewhere in the melee I had lost Mama's shoes. I began laughing. Sam looked over at me with a curious look. I just kept laughing. "Girl, what the hell is you laughing at?" Sam asked.

"We put it on them girls. I can't believe Sharmaine put her hands on me."

"Who was that girl anyway and where do you know her from?" Sam asked.

"She used to go to middle school with me. I haven't seen her in years. She was always jealous of me in school. She and some of her friends followed me home one day talking trash. I guess she thought it was cool to put her hands on me tonight. She won't put her hands on nobody else, I bet that."

"Yeah girl, you messed her up bad and LaWanda was on Rene before I could move so I just grabbed the next trick in line," Sam said laughing.

We laughed and replayed the fight over and over, each time remembering another detail. We all went back to my house and sat on the porch. Sam rolled up two more joints and Toya got some beers out of the cooler in the trunk of her car. We sat on the porch smoking, drinking, and laughing until five-thirty in the morning. Sam said she had to get the car home so she left. I made her promise to call me when she got home, I wanted to make sure she got home okay. I know we were all buzzing. LaWanda, Toya, and I went in the house and I straightened up while Wanda and Toya slept. Sam called me and let me know she had made it home okay.

I finally got in my bed at quarter to seven. I laid there looking up at my ceiling thinking about the night before. We never got into Topics and Kevin never got to ask me out. Mama woke me up around one-thirty that afternoon. My head was pounding. Mama stood in the doorway to my room.

"Lucinda, you hear me ?!"

I tried to get my eyes to focus as I sat up in my bed. "Ma'am?"

"This little black boy out here on my porch asking for you." I wiped my eyes.

"Ma'am?"

"Girl, get ya behind up and see what this little black boy want. What you doing sleep this late in the afternoon anyway? What you did last night? I know you ain't have no boys in my house."

"No ma'am," I said easing out of bed. "I went to the movies with Samantha," I said, hoping LaWanda hadn't said anything different.

"Well, you need to see who this little boy on my porch is. He black as I don't know what. You like them dark ones don't you ?"

"Mama!"

"Hurry up and go see who this is, he been here three times already and what happened to your face?"

I felt a quick shot of fear run up my spine thinking I was busted. "Sam made a mistake and scratched me when we was playing, is it bad?"

Mama grasped my chin between her index finger and thumb and twist my face to the right. "It ain't nothing but a scratch but put some cocoa butter on it."

I followed behind Mama trying to peep around her to see who was on the porch. She said a little black boy. I was wondering who could it be. Sometimes a few of the boys I hung out with in the neighborhood would stop by to see how I was doing, but she said this boy had been here three times already. Mama opened the front door and pushed open the screen. I walked out onto the porch, the wood felt cool on my bare feet. I saw Kevin sitting on the swing. He began to smile. I smiled too, hoping Mama didn't follow me outside. "Lucinda you ain't going to introduce me to your friend?"

"Yes ma'am," I said rolling my eyes in my head. "Kevin, this is my mother Ms. Mary. Mama, this is Kevin."

"How you doing ma'am?" Kevin said.

"Didn't she just tell you my name was Ms. Mary? I'm fine, Kevin, how are you?" Mama said with a hint of a smile.

"Mama!" I said, turning to face her.

"What?" Mama said, stepping out onto the porch. "So where you live Kevin?"

"I live up the street in that green house around the curve, Ms. Mary" Kevin said with a smile.

"You smiling a lot Kevin, you like my daughter?" "Mama!" I screamed, I felt so embarrassed.

"Yes, ma'am... I mean Ms. Mary."

Mama looked at me and smiled. "Make sure you treat her like a young lady. That's what she is." Mama stepped back in the house and closed the door.

I felt relieved. I wasn't sure if it was because Mama had went back in the house or if Kevin had finally admitted he liked me. I didn't know what to say. I walked over to the swing and sat down next to Kevin. "Hey Kev."

"Hey slugger," Kevin said smiling at me.

I smiled. "What?" I said, pretending not to know what he was talking about.

"That was crazy last night. Ya'll really beat Rene and those other girls down. Who was that girl that got up in your face? I never saw her at school."

"She don't go to Glenn Hills. I know her from my junior high school. Her name is Sharmaine. She was always jealous of me when we were in school. I can't believe she put her hands in my face like that."

"Yeah, you snapped. Ya'll almost started a riot out there last night." I touched a finger to the scratch on my face. "I hope this doesn't leave a scar."

Kevin touched his fingers to the scratch and smiled, "It won't. It's just a scratch."

His fingers felt so soft and soothing against my face. I was disappointed when he pulled his hand back. "So you came over here because you was concerned about me. My mother said you been here two times already."

"I'm always concerned about you. Plus I saw Toya and Wanda going to work earlier. They told me to come check on you."

I had forgot that LaWanda had to work today. I know she must be at work feeling terrible. I was happy to be sitting here with Kevin, but my head was pounding. I think this is what they called a hangover. "Yeah, I think Sam had to work today, too."

"So what are you going to do today?"

"I'm probably going to climb back in bed and sleep until about five o'clock."

"You want to go to the movies later?" "You asking me out?"

"Yes, in more ways than one."

"What that mean, in more ways than on?"

"Come on, Cinda. You know I like you. I like you a lot. Why don't you go out with me?"

I smiled. Sam might have been right. "Because you haven't asked me to go out with you."

"I just did."

"No you didn't. You asked me why I won't go out with

# Finding Daddy

you?" I said, smiling.

"So why won't you?"

"I just told you, because you haven't asked me."

"Girl you crazy. So are you going to be my girlfriend?"

"I don't know if you are ready for that Kevin. You got a lot of little football fans at school that wear skirts and go crazy every time you touch the ball."

"I ain't thinking about those girls. I know who I like and what I want."

I raised an eyebrow. "And what do you want?" "I want your friendship, I want to hold your hand, I want to go to the movies with you. I want you to make me smile."

If Kevin was running game, he had me. I was feeling all warm inside and I felt my heart rate speed up. Just as I was about to answer him, Mama appeared in the doorway. "Lucinda, Samantha just called and said if you want a job you need to get downtown before four o'clock."

I jumped up off the swing and let out a high pitched scream. I was so excited I started heading back in the house behind Mama. Sam had came through. She said she was going to get me that job. This was turning out to be a great day. I got a job and Kevin asked me out. Kevin! I was so excited I almost left him sitting on the swing. "Congratulations Cinda. I'm suppose to start working at Albertson's on Monday."

"Oh, for real?" I said pausing at the doorway. "Which one?"

"The same one your sister works at."

"That is so cool. Listen Kev, I gotta take a shower and get ready; I can't miss this job."

"I know. So are you going to answer my question." "Yes."

"Is that your answer?"

"Yes, yes, yes. Call me later. I'll let you know how the interview went." I stepped inside the house before Kevin could respond. If I stood there looking at his fine, black self, I probably would've never left the porch.

"So, Samantha got you an interview at her job?"

"Yes, she said she would." I was so happy. A job meant independence. I mean the support check was good but I always wanted to make my own money. I watched Mama work and move us out the projects. There was no telling what I could do with a job. I felt so good I wanted to shout.

Mama must have seen it too. She was smiling as hard as me. "You need me to drop you off downtown?"

"Yes Mama, will you ?"

"Yeah, I'll drop you off. I might go by your Nana's house today since I finally got a day off."

"Okay, let me get ready. I might can stop by and see Nana for a minute if we get out of here quick enough."

I took a shower and got dressed. I put on a crisp white blouse, a navy blue skirt, and a blue Caryssa leather pump. I curled my hair and clipped my nails. By the time I slipped my blue blazer over my shoulders, I was feeling like a corporate attorney. Even Mama was impressed. "Now you look like a young lady ready to conquer the world. Have you seen my black open toe sandals? I was going to let you wear them but I can't find them. It doesn't matter. You picked a much better shoe. You ready ?"

"Yes."

"Put some cocoa butter on that scratch on your face. You need to be more careful when you playing around. Women don't wear scars and blemishes well."

"Yes, ma'am."

I put the cocoa butter on my face and we left. Mama quizzed me all the way to Nana's about Kevin. Where did I meet him? How long did I know him? Did I like him? I felt so embarrassed talking to my mother about Kevin. She said he seemed nice, but he was just so black. I loved Kevin's dark chocolate skin tone. I liked everything about Kevin. Then Mama gave me her be careful speech; the same one she had given LaWanda when she had found that baseball cap in her room. We made it to Nana's house around two-thirty. She was sitting out on the porch with her friend, Ms. Grace from down the street. Nana and Ms. Grace would sit on the porch most of the day and talk about the goings on in the neighborhood. Ms. Grace would sit there chewing her snuff, spitting into a can and serving up gossip to Nana. I didn't know at

the time how much of a drama queen Nana was. "Hey Mary, which one is that them girls of yours getting so big?" Ms. Grace said, as me and Mama entered the screened-in porch.

## Finding Daddy

"That's my baby, Lucinda. Where you going all dressed up young lady?" Nana asked.

"I got a job interview, Nana." I said, giving her a peck on the cheek.

"Oh really, where at?"

"At the Woolworth's downtown."

"That's good. I hope you get the job. You definitely looking good."

"Thank you, Nana. I should get the job. My friend Samantha works there and she talked to the supervisor for me."

"How you gonna get back and forth downtown everyday? You know your Mama going to be working during the week. That bus line is so crazy you can't depend on that. Why don't you see if your Uncle Clarence can drop you off during the week? You can get off your school bus over here and Clarence can run you downtown. Clarence!" Nana screamed from the porch.

I started to protest. I didn't even know if I had the job or not, or what my schedule was going to be. But Nana had already had everything figured out and Mama had told us once Nana made up her mind about something you just let it go. My Uncle Clarence appeared in the doorway to the house with a brown skinned woman I had never seen before; his right arm was wrapped around her waist and she had a bright smile on her face. "Yes ma'am, you called me?" Uncle Clarence asked. Stepping out onto the porch he gave my mother a hug and stepped back and looked at me. "Hey, Cinda. What you all dressed up for?"

"She got a job interview down at that Woolworth's downtown, and if she get the job, she going to need you to take her to work during the week."

"Congratulations, Cinda. You know I'll run you to work. I want ya'll to meet somebody," Uncle Clarence said, signaling to the woman in the doorway to come out on the porch. "This is my friend, Janet. Janet, this is my sister Mary and my niece Lucinda."

"Hey, nice to meet you," Janet said.

Me and Mama spoke and I asked Uncle Clarence if he had any lemonade in the house. I loved the way my uncle Clarence made lemonade. I would sometimes drink a whole pitcher when I came over. I went into the house and made a tall glass of lemonade and started back out to the porch. As I got closer to the door, I heard Mama's voice and she sounded upset.

"Do you know this woman had the nerve to call my house. She telling me how they bringing Robert up before a review board and considering discharging him because I lied to the people at the hospital and told them I was Robert's wife. I told her I didn't tell them white folks nothing at that hospital. I was in labor. Robert told them people that. I don't care if they discharge him or not, he is going to take care of his responsibility. I told her I don't have to lie on Robert. The judge and a DNA test proved who the liar was. I told that woman not to call my house no more with that nonsense and hung up on her."

"I told you years ago 'bout that Robert. He a run-around man. He fall in love with every woman he meet until he see the next one. A man like that just ain't nothing! You should be happy to be rid of that no good bastard," Nana said.

I couldn't believe they were talking about my daddy. Mama never talked about daddy with me and what lady was she talking about? Why were they trying to discharge daddy because we were his girls? I walked out onto the porch and Ms. Grace tapped Nana's leg. My Uncle Clarence offered me a ride downtown to Woolworth's. I really wanted Mama to take me. I wanted to ask her about daddy, but I could tell Mama wasn't in no mood to go anywhere by the look on her face.

"What you got in there to taste, Clarence?" Mama asked.

"I got some Seagram's gin in there under my nightstand in the room. Come on, Janet, ride down here with me."

Janet, Uncle Clarence, and I piled into his Toyota Cressida and we headed downtown. I sat in the backseat thinking about the things I had heard my Mama and Nana saying. Why hadn't my daddy called? Was this lady the reason my daddy hadn't come back like he said he would? I felt the tears burning at my eyes but I refused to cry. I was going to get this job and be independent. My Uncle Clarence wasn't paying me any mind. He was busy in the front seat talking to his friend Janet. He barely said goodbye when he dropped me off and pulled away from the curb. I walked into the five and dime store with my head held high. I was determined to get this job. I didn't see Sam when I walked in. There were three cashiers at the front of the store. I stepped to the middle register because there was only one customer in her line. I waited until she

# Finding Daddy

was done dealing with the customer, then I stepped up and smiled. The cashier was a middle aged white woman with a blond dye job pulled in a ponytail and a thick coat of red lipstick. I noticed a tiny red spot from the lipstick on her teeth when she smiled. "Can I help you?"

I realized that Sam hadn't given me the name of the supervisor. I looked around nervously for Sam. I felt my palms starting to sweat, then I just spoke. "I'm looking for the manager, I'm here to interview for a job."

The cashier, whose name tag read "Jenny," maintained her smile as she spoke, "Well, honey you must be looking for Rochelle over in the dining area, that's the only position I know that's open right now. Just go up this aisle and take a left. Good luck."

"Thank you," I followed the directions the woman had given me and I saw Sam standing behind the dining counter. I approached with relief. "Hey."

"Hey girl, you made it. You look good. Rochelle in the back. She'll be out in a minute. You want something to eat while you wait?"

"No thank you. I will take a Slush Puppie though," I said with a smile.

"I got you girl."

"So how's the supervisor?"

"Who Rochelle? She cool. Don't worry girl, you definitely going to get the job. We might have different schedules though."

"That's cool. My uncle can bring me on the days we don't ride together. So how did you sleep?"

"I barely slept. Me and mom sat up talking about the fight. We really did a number on those chicks. You alright?"

I couldn't believe it. Sam had went home and talked to her moms about the fight. How cool is that? Mama would've had a fit, wanting to go talk to kids' parents and everything. "Yeah I'm cool. I just got this little scratch," I said, fingering the scratch with my index finger. "Guess what?"

"What?"

"Kevin came to my house this morning." "For real? What he say?"

"He said we messed them chicks up. He had been to my house two times before Mama woke me up."

"I told you, girl. That boy want you."

"I know," I said, with a sly smile. "He asked me to be his girlfriend."

"What you say, girl?"

I smiled so hard my cheeks were hurting. "I said, yes."

"I knew you was going to crack. You should've made him sweat."

A pretty brunette came from the back carrying a clipboard. "Sam, are you harassing the customers again?" the woman said with a smile.

"Naw, this one's harassing me. This Lucinda."

"Oh, my new counter person. How you doing? Rochelle," She said, coming toward me extending her right hand.

"Hello. Lucinda."

"You going to like working here. We have a lot of fun. I'm sure Sam told you. We usually just work the dining area. You'll just get customers menus and write down their orders when they decide on what they want. You'll clip the slips on that ring over there," Rochelle said, pointing over her shoulder at the silver ring hanging above a metal counter situated between the kitchen area and the area where Rochelle and Sam stood. "Once you clip the order, Dave and Linda, they are the cooks and I'll introduce you to them in a minute. But they will take the slips and tell you when the order is up. You'll get your five dollar hourly wage and tips. So does Woolworth's sound like someplace you would like to work?"

I smiled. "Yes."

"Did you bring all your paperwork?"

"Yes ma'am," I said, digging in my purse and pulling out my working papers, social security card, birth certificate, and school I.D.

"I already told you, you have the job, honey, you don't have to keep calling me ma'am," Rochelle said smiling. "Why don't you come around the counter so I can show you around," Rochelle said, taking my paperwork and clipping it to the clipboard.

Rochelle took me on a tour of the dining area and introduced me to the cooks. She made me a name tag and gave me the burgundy shirt that passed for the store's uniform. I met the other workers in the store as we toured the main floor and then we went back to the dining area to an office in the back where I

## Finding Daddy

completed the application and some other paperwork. Rochelle gave me my schedule and asked if I had a way to work on the days Sam couldn't bring me. I told her about my uncle and ensured her the schedule wasn't a problem. I decided to wait for Sam after my interview since she was clocking out about fifteen minutes after Rochelle and I finished up. I called Nana and spoke to Mama. I could tell she was tipsy as soon as she got on the phone. She kept asking me if I got the job and if I needed her to come pick me up. I finally got her attention long enough to let her know I didn't need a ride and I would be home later. I was going to ask Sam if she wanted to go to the movies with Kevin and me. I hadn't forgotten his invitation from earlier. In fact I had been thinking about it ever since Rochelle had told me I had the job.

Sam came out the store twenty minutes later carrying two cherry Slush Puppies.

"I couldn't wait to get out of there. So how you like Rochelle?" "She seems cool."

"She is, girl, and guess what?"

"She likes brothers," Sam said laughing. "Girl stop lying."

"I swear to God," Sam said, raising her right hand.

I joined her laughter. I didn't know too many white women that dated black men back then. We got in the Mustang and Sam headed toward the freeway. "So you want to go to the movies with me and Kevin tonight?"

"Dang girl, ya'll just started going out this morning and ya'll already going to the movies? I hope he paying."

"Of course he is...for me," I said laughing.

Sam laughed and gave me a high five. "Well, let me get home and take a shower and get out these clothes. I'll check my little black book and see who I feel like being around."

Sam was so cool to me. She was so confident. She knew guys wanted to get with her and she made them sweat. I was confident, too, but in a different way. I was confident in the fact that I was going to succeed in life. Sam seemed to live carefree and still keep it all in control. When Sam got off the highway, we stopped at Church's and got a snack box. I told Sam to drop me off at home so I could change. I told her I would call her later. Soon as I got in the house I got out of my clothes and jumped in the shower. Soon as I got out of the shower, I got dressed and called Kevin. On the third ring a woman answered, "Hello."

"Hello, may I speak to Kevin, please." "May I ask who's calling?"

"Lucinda."

"Hold on. Kevin! Kevin come get this phone, it's for you." After a few seconds Kevin came on the line sounding out of breath. "Hello."

"Hello. Why you breathing so hard? Let me find out you ran to the phone, who was you expecting a call from?"

"Hey Cinda. I was just working out. What's up?"

"I was just calling to see if you still was paying my way to the movies tonight?" I said, thinking about what Sam had said earlier.

"I got you. You know that. Hold on a minute." I heard Kevin talking to someone in the background. "Hey Lucinda, can you come over here for a minute? My mom wants to meet you."

I was stuck for a second, I didn't know what to say. "Okay." "Alright. Are you leaving your house now?"

"Give me like, ten minutes."

"Alright. Take the path in the back of your house. It will lead you to the back of my house. I'll meet you on the top of the hill there."

"Okay. Kevin ?" "Yeah."

"How you know about that path?"

"Girl, I been living in this neighborhood for twelve years. Ain't a cut I don't know."

"Okay. I'll meet you there."

I hung up with Kevin and pulled my Levi's out my drawer. I quickly ironed them and slipped them on with a black stretch shirt. I put on my black Reebok classics and put on my black butter soft leather. The afternoon air had gotten cool and I felt a breeze when Sam dropped me off. I didn't have time to call Sam. I told Kevin I would meet him in ten minutes and I wasn't really even sure where this path was. I made sure the front door was locked and went out the back door. I was only able to lock the bottom lock on the back door because I didn't have the key for the top lock. Rusty met me at the back door barking and jumping against my leg. I calmed him with a pat to the head and a stroke of his ear. I stepped off the back porch and Rusty followed alongside me until I

## Finding Daddy

exited the backside of our fence. Rusty whimpered as I looked for the path in the evening dusk. The wind had picked up, too.

I finally found the path off to the right. I followed it until it came to a split, one side kept going into the gloaming and the other led up a small hill. I heard someone coming down the hill and then someone in a dark colored hooded sweatshirt appeared. The hood was pulled over their head blocking a clear view to their face. I froze up then my nerves caused me to go in defense mode. I threw up my hands in a defense as the figure reached for me. "You still trying to fight, girl. I don't want no problems," Kevin said pulling the hood from his head.

I took his hand and we started back up the hill. "Boy, I was about to knock you silly."

"I saw that," Kevin said laughing. "Is your mother mean?"

"No. Why you ask that?"

"Just want to know what I'm walking into."

"My mother didn't really want to meet you. I just couldn't talk to you with her looking over my shoulder, besides I wanted to see you. You upset with me?"

We stopped at the top of the hill near a big tree. "No, I'm not upset with you. I'm glad you told me about this path. I wanted to see you, too."

We sat up there on that hill talking for hours. The night had brought on a frigid chill and our noses were running. We talked about everything. He talked to me about his family, his mother and father, and his little sister. I talked to him about LaWanda and Mama and my dad. I really opened up to him about my dad and how I felt. I told him the things I had heard my Nana and Mama talking about earlier that day. It was the first time I had really opened up to anyone about how I felt about my dad. For some reason I just felt like I could trust Kevin. I didn't know it then but this spot on the hill under the big tree would become our "meeting spot" on many occasions; our sharing space, our caring space, our loving space, or what we thought was love back then.

We never made it to the movies that night, but we seen plenty of movies together. We became almost inseparable. On Mondays in school we would hear our names over the school intercom system calling off our individual stats for the week before. Sam, Kevin, and I were always mentioned. I didn't have any problems with the girls on my softball team anymore. When we came back to school after the brawl at the gas station, Rene and her crew stood clear of me. I never heard anything about Sharmaine again. It always seemed to be Sam, Kevin and me. LaWanda had finally saved up enough money and bought her own car, a blue Chevy Corsica. When Sam couldn't get away from work (she had got a new job setting up banquets for fancy parties), we would pile into the Cosica on Friday nights and head to the school football games. LaWanda was dating a linebacker on the varsity team named Tyrone. He was a senior, too. He was going away to med school after graduation on a full sports scholarship. It was so cool because Tyrone and Kevin knew each other from the team. So me and LaWanda started hanging again. But it was mostly Sam, Kevin and I.

I did finally meet Kevin's mother and father, Mr. and Mrs. Roberts. They were so cool. His little sister Angela adored me. I started spending a lot of time at Kevin's house. One Sunday we all sat around and watched *The Wiz*. Angela kept cuddling close to me every time the witch would appear. Kevin, Angela, and I crowded the loveseat; it felt like a real family setting. Mr. and Mrs. Roberts watched the movie like it was their first time seeing it. They laughed and commented on the costumes used for the characters. Later on that night when we had dinner, we all joined hands and Mr. Roberts let me lead the prayer. I was so nervous. I bowed my head and closed my eyes.

"God bless our lives with patience and grace. May the food we take in feed us with the need to do your will. Amen."

I opened my eyes when I heard everybody say, "Amen." Mrs. Roberts was looking at me with a big smile on her face. "That was beautiful, Lucinda."

"Thank you." I felt so special. I never forgot that day. I learned so much spending time with Kevin and his family. I felt a strong sense of family values when I was with them. The one thing I really liked about spending time with them was that it always felt like family. They always ate dinner together and they always set aside time throughout the week for family night. Sometimes we would play board games like Monopoly, or just sit around and talk.They made me feel so comfortable, like I was part of the family.

## Finding Daddy

As the school year came to an end, Kevin kept telling me he had a surprise for me. He had a bright look in his eyes every time he brought it up, but he wouldn't tell me what it was. He wouldn't even give me a clue. I would try to wheedle it out of him during our late night conversations. I remember Mrs. Roberts would always be trying to call on the other line and Kevin would never click over to answer her call. She worked as a nurse at the hospital at night and she would be calling trying to check on Angela. I would hear Mr. Roberts telling Kevin to answer the other line if it rang. Sometimes Mrs. Roberts would put Kevin on phone restriction and at those times we would meet on the path on top of the hill. During the winter months, it would be cold and I would bundle up real good in my goose coat. We would sit out there for hours in the darkness just talking and laughing and expressing puppy love for each other. I could still smell the outside air on my clothing when I came in from the path.

LaWanda, Toya, and Sam were getting ready for graduation. Most of the senior class was going to Cancun for their graduation trip. I was so envious watching LaWanda and the others shop for bathing suits and other sun-fun accessories. I couldn't wait until it was my turn to graduate. Kevin was graduating, too but he wasn't going on the trip with the rest of the seniors. He said he'd rather spend time with me. That was so sweet. Sam was still putting me on to what game to watch for with boys. A lot of females were really jealous that me and Kevin were dating and Kevin liked the attention. It began to cause some problems, but I remained a lady and didn't have to put my hands on nobody this time. Right before graduation, me and Kevin were in the mall browsing and just hanging out. We walked into Foot Locker and trying on a pair of tennis shoes was Sam. What shocked us was who she was with. Tyrone was sitting next to her helping her tie the shoe and their demeanor was that of a couple. Sam looked up and saw me staring at her and Tyrone. I just walked out of the store and Kevin followed behind me. I knew the type of girl Sam was...she was my best friend. There was no doubt in my mind something was going on between her and Tyrone. "Why didn't you say something?"

I stopped walking. "What was I suppose to say? I just saw my best friend with my sister's boyfriend."

"Well maybe they were just hanging out."

"Come on Kevin! I just told you that is my best friend and you know your boy."

"What's that suppose to mean?"

"I don't know, Kevin. I don't know nothing right now. I'm going to catch the bus home."

"Come on, Cinda, don't be like that. Why are we fighting?"

I touched a palm to Kevin's face. "We're not. I just need to be alone. I'll call you later. I promise."

"You sure you alright, Cinda?"

"I'm fine," I said lying. I walked away and disappeared into the crowd. I heard Tyrone calling after me but I never turned around. What was I going to do? How was I going to tell LaWanda this? How was I going to tell Mama? She liked Sam, especially after she had got me that job. Why did Sam have to mess with Tyrone? She knew he was off limits. We had all hung out together at the movies, we'd gone to eat. The more I thought about it, the more upset I got. It was like she had deliberately disrespected me. I had looked up to her. Had our friendship meant nothing to her all this time ? I got on the bus and walked to the back and sat next to the window. I stared out the window all the way to my stop. I felt heart broken. I got off the bus and walked to the neighborhood. I prayed LaWanda was at work or out with Toya somewhere. I walked around the curve that came around by our driveway and was relieved to see the driveway empty. I walked up the gravel path and onto the porch. I unlocked the door and walked in the house. I didn't bother turning on any lights. I walked to my room shut the door behind me and crawled in my bed.

I awoke to the ringing of the phone on the nightstand next to my bed. My room was bathed in darkness and I was a little disoriented. I reached out to the phone and lifted the receiver off the cradle. "Hello."

"Hey, sweetness."

"Hey." It was Kevin. I felt bad about leaving him in the mall earlier, but it felt good to hear his voice.

"How you feeling?"

"I'm alright. I'm sorry for taking off like that." "It's cool. I understand. Did you talk to Sam?" "No!"

"What about LaWanda?"

## Finding Daddy

"No. I don't even know what I'm going to tell her." "I'm sure Tyrone probably talked to her by now." "What did he say to you?"

"They admitted they had been messing around for about a month."

"A month! Sam told you that?"

"They both did. I think Sam was hurt that you caught her and not your sister. She kept saying she was sorry. Are you going to forgive her?"

I hadn't really thought about it. Was I going to forgive her? "I don't know."

"You know that's your girl."

"Yes, but Wanda is my sister. She knew that Tyrone was with LaWanda." I felt tears starting to burn my eyes again. "I just need to think. I'll call you back later."

"Why don't you come meet me on the path ?" "Not right now, Kevin. I just need to think."

"Well I wasn't going to tell you but my mother bought the tickets today."

"What tickets?"

"The plane tickets to Seattle." "Seattle?"

"Yes. That's where I'm going the week after graduation. My Aunt Kim lives out there. Have you ever been out west?"

"No." I was wondering how I was going to convince Mama to let me go. Mama liked Kevin, but going away with him to another coast. I didn't think Mama was going to let me go. I wished we were leaving tomorrow the way I was feeling. I just wanted to get away. I needed to think about what I was going to do about Sam and how I was going to face my own sister. I felt sick. "Kevin I'll call you in a little while. I just got to think."

"Call me, please. I'm here for you. I miss you."

"I miss you, too." I hung up the phone and rolled over onto my back. I stared into the darkness. What was I going to do? Samantha was like my sister too, but LaWanda *was* my sister. I squeezed my eyes shut, my head was starting to hurt. The ring from the phone pulled me from my thoughts. I reached out for the phone and picked it up. "Hello." There was a long pause then I heard someone breathe into the other end of the line. "Hello." I said again. Just as I was about to put the phone on the receiver, I

~ 131 ~

heard someone say something. I pulled the phone back close to my ear, "Hello!"

"Hey."

I couldn't believe it. It was Sam. Her tone was nonchalant. I didn't know what to say. My mouth was suddenly dry and my heart began to beat against my chest. "Hello." I said, again trying to stall so I could get my thoughts together.

"Hello!" This time Sam's voice sounded a little agitated.

"Yes," I said, not knowing what else to say.

"I know you are probably upset with me, and it's understandable. I just want you to know it wasn't personal against you or LaWanda. I'm sorry. I know blood's thicker than water. That's your sister. I was just somebody you was cool with." Then she hung up. I just sat there with the phone pressed to my ear, not noticing the constant buzzing of the line. I finally hung the phone up and sat up in my bed. What had just happened? Did Sam just end our friendship? I felt hurt and confused. I was wondering how I was going to tell Sam we couldn't be friends anymore. Now that she had called and basically told me our friendship was over, I felt empty. It took a long time for me to recover from that phone call. I felt abandoned and I made up my mind right then and there I wasn't going to let anybody else in my life leave me. I began crying thinking about what had just happened with Sam. I started thinking about my daddy and how he had left. I finally got out my bed and got on my knees and began praying. I hope my father heard me.

# CHAPTER 10
## LAWANDA'S GRADUATION

LaWanda was graduating in less than a week. She was excited and I was excited for her. All I kept thinking about was my graduation and what I was going to do. It had been two months since I had seen Tyrone and Sam together. I hadn't spoken to Sam since the night she called me and told me that blood was thicker than water and to stand by my sister. I learned a valuable lesson from that incident. I was never going to let anyone get close to me again. I refused to be hurt like that again. I was determined to hurt someone before they hurt me. LaWanda had gotten over Tyrone pretty quickly and she was dating Darren Holt, the center for the varsity basketball team. When I told her about Tyrone and Sam, she had said she already knew. She said Tyrone had come to her job and confessed. She said he had begged her to forgive him, but she had cut him off on the spot. Besides, she had started thinking Darren was cute and she was ready to be rid of Tyrone. I didn't know how to feel when she told me that. It was like I had lost my best friend over nothing. I reasoned with myself though that it wasn't for nothing. Sam had violated regardless of how LaWanda felt about Tyrone. He was supposed to be off limits to her and anyone else we hung with.

The incident with Tyrone and Sam affected me in such a way that it began to interfere with my relationship with Kevin. I had crawled into a shell and I didn't want to come out. We still hung out and did things together, but it was different now. I didn't really want to be in a relationship anymore. I didn't want to be close to anyone anymore. I was more excited about LaWanda graduating than I was about going to Seattle with Kevin. Mama had finally agreed to let me go with Kevin and his family. She said it was only fair since LaWanda was going away to Cancun. Besides, Mama liked Kevin and after she talked to his parents she decided to let me go with them. LaWanda and I had just left the mall. We were grabbing some last minute items for our trips. LaWanda pulled into the travel agency parking lot. When we walked in, I couldn't believe my eyes. Sam was sitting with one of the travel agents at a desk. She looked up at us as we entered and turned her attention back to the agent. She hadn't even given me a curt nod. I had seen her in school several times after the phone call. She had never spoken or acknowledged me in school. I didn't know why I was expecting her to speak to me now, but I did. LaWanda seemed unfazed by Sam's presence and stepped up to the next available agent's desk. I took a seat in the front and tried not to look in the direction Sam was sitting but I couldn't help it.

"Hello. May I help you?" the agent asked LaWanda.

"Yes. I'm here to pay my balance and confirm my reservations."

"Okay. How many people are in your party and what's the name?"

"My name is LaWanda Wilson. I'm with the graduating class from Glenn Hills."

The agent typed something on her keyboard and read the screen. "Okay, I've got you right here. Your class is going to Cancun. Your balance is three hundred and sixty seven dollars and I'm going to need to get a copy of your passport. Do you have it with you today?"

"Yes ma'am, I do," LaWanda said, getting the cash and passport out of her purse and handing it to the agent.

"Okay, just let me get a copy of your passport and I will give you your receipt and confirmation packet."

"Okay, thank you."

I was sitting there feeling so uncomfortable. Just a few short months ago we had all been hanging out together laughing and being supportive of each other. Now we were sitting in the same room and avoiding eye contact. Sam got up from the desk where she was sitting with the agent and gathered her things to leave. I heard LaWanda huff as Sam passed by her. Sam just kept walking without a backward glance. She stared right into my eyes as she walked past me and out the door. I couldn't help myself, I turned my head and watched as she walked to her mother's BMW. When she got to the car, she opened the door and looked at me

## Finding Daddy

through the window pane of the agency before ducking into the car. "Skank." I heard LaWanda say.

I turned around and began to stare at the clock on the wall at the back of the agency. I just wanted to get out of here. I was supposed to be meeting Kevin in a couple of hours to go to the movies. I didn't know if I was up to it anymore because I was feeling empty again. I just wanted to go home and get in my bed. The agent brought LaWanda her receipt and packet back and we left.

When we got in the car, LaWanda said she wanted to go get something to eat real quick before she met Toya. They were going to a senior's beach party later on. They had invited me but I had already made plans with Kevin. Now, I just wanted to go home and relax my mind. I didn't feel like being bothered. We stopped at Church's, grabbed a couple of snack boxes, and went home. "Did you see that nasty skank in there?" LaWanda asked sitting down next to me on the couch.

I knew she was talking about Sam. "Yeah, I saw her. She was probably paying her balance, too."

"Umm huh. I wonder who man she's going to try and wrangle away. She couldn't even look at me and now Tyrone is messing with Sheila McKinnley. I know she feels so stupid."

"Probably not."

"What you mean?" LaWanda said giving me a funny look.

I didn't really know how to explain to LaWanda that Sam probably was done with Tyrone the minute she rolled over. That was just her way. LaWanda and Toya had been around us but they hadn't hung with us. Wanda didn't really know Sam like I did. "She's just like that. To her she's not even looking at it like she's being fast or easy. To her it's a conquest she sets her mind to do something and once she feels satisfied with it, she moves on. Tyrone was just something to do at the time."

LaWanda looked at me and rolled her eyes. "You really think that? That girl is just loose. Whatever, I just hope you don't think it's okay to be jumping from boy to boy."

LaWanda had just offended me with her last statement. She knew better than anybody that I wasn't loose. Had she forgotten she was the one who had broken up with Tyrone and started dating Darren? She didn't seem all that broken up about it, in fact I seemed to be the one most affected by my sister's boyfriend messing with my best friend. "The way Sam feels about how she handles her business with guys is her preference. I respect myself. No one can influence me to do something I don't want to." I got up from the couch and left LaWanda sitting there. I went in my room and shut the door. I laid across my bed and exhaled. I heard a knock on the door. "Come in."

LaWanda walked and sat on the bed. "I'm sorry, Cinda. I guess I'm just a little upset at the fact that I don't know what Tyrone saw in her that he didn't see in me."

"It's alright, LaWanda, I understand. He probably wasn't looking for anything in her other than what she offered. He lost out and we learned a lesson."

"We?"

"Yes. I learned that friends are not the people that you spend most of your time with but the people that you find the most common ground with. I really did like Sam, but the truth is I liked the things about her that I never saw myself doing. In a way I guess I might have even been a little jealous of her personality. There were times when I did want to do the things she was doing, but a part of me always held back. That was my true self stepping in the shadow of influence."

LaWanda rubbed a palm along my back. "I love you, Cinda. I'm so glad you are my sister."

"Me too," I said sitting up laughing.

"Why don't you come hang out with us tonight?"

"I told you, I already made plans to go to the movies with Kevin."

"I know, but you are going to be with him for a whole week in Seattle in a couple of weeks, plus ya'll can go to the movies tomorrow after you get off work. I'll drop ya'll off and come back and get you. I really want to hang out with my little sister tonight."

LaWanda really had me choked up. It had been a long time since LaWanda wanted to actually hang out with me. I really wanted to hang out with her tonight too. I was feeling better; I wasn't stressing anymore. "Let me call Kevin and cancel. I'm going to hang out with ya'll tonight."

"Alright, let me go get in the shower."

I dialed Kevin's number and Ms. Roberts picked up on the

# Finding Daddy

third ring. "Hello."

"Hello. Hey Ms. Roberts." "Hey Cinda, how you doing?" "I'm alright and you?"

"I'm fine just tired. I'm about to lie down and get some much needed rest. Are you ready to go to Seattle?"

"Yes ma'am."

"I think you are going to like it. It rains a lot out there but we should still be able to get out and see the sights. Besides, my sister has a nice big house with a rec room and home theater in the basement. How's your mother?"

"She's alright, working."

"That lady know she love to work."

"Yeah, she's trying to get as many hours as she can. She says she wants to buy a house. I just hope we move to a house in the neighborhood."

"Oh okay, she's trying to buy a home. That's good. There's some nice houses for sale in the neighborhood. Why don't you start taking down some of the numbers of the realtors while your mom is at work?"

"That's a good idea. I'm going to start doing that."

"Yeah, let me know what you come up with. I'll help you. We'll find your mom a nice house right here in the neighborhood. Hold on, let me get Kevin."

I heard Ms. Roberts call for Kevin and a few minutes later he came on the line. "Hey Cinda, what's up?"

"Nothing really, I just wanted to ask you do you mind going to the movies tomorrow night? LaWanda wants me to go with her to the beach party."

"The one the seniors are having?" "Yeah."

"Why didn't you say you wanted to go, we could've went there instead. I am a senior, you know."

"It's not like that. I wasn't planning on going to the party. It's just that LaWanda really wants to hang out with me tonight. It's a sister thing. You don't mind do you? Wanda said she would drop us off at the movies tomorrow and pick us back up."

There was a long silence. "I understand. Hang out with your sister, we'll do something some other time. I'll talk to you later. Have fun."

"Okay. Are you going to come to the party?" "I don't know.

I might."

"I'll be looking for you." "I'm not sure I'm coming." "Alright."

"Alright." "Kevin?" "Yes."

"Thank you for being so understanding." "Of course, what did you expect?"

I felt so good. I was going to hang out with my older sister. I finally felt free of the feelings that had been clouding my heart since Sam told me we were no longer friends. I began getting my clothes out for my shower. I felt like dancing. I eased into Mama's room and got the bottle of gin from her room closet. I went into the kitchen and took out two glasses and made LaWanda and me a drink. LaWanda came from her room with a joint pressed tightly between her lips. She lit the tip of the joint and blew a cloud of smoke in my direction. I smiled. It was so ironic how I had gone to get the gin and Wanda had came with the joint. I held up her glass and exchanged it for the joint. I pulled on the marijuana stick and felt the smoke fill up my lungs, but I didn't cough as I exhaled. I had started smoking a lot more since that first night. I even had my own stash rolled up in a pair of socks in my dresser. "This is the best thing that broad did for me." LaWanda said, taking the joint back from me and hitting it. Wanda closed her left eye so the smoke from the joint wouldn't go in it as the marijuana smoke drifted upward. "Giving me her weed connect. That's the best thing she could've done."

I began to giggle. "I know that's right." I said offering LaWanda a high five. "I'm going to take my shower real quick. Put the gin back in Mama's room." "Okay. Hurry up cause I gotta curl my hair."

After I got out the shower, I decided to roll a joint out of my stash and surprise LaWanda. No one knew about my stash and I had never smoked in the house before today. I always walked to the path in the back of the house. Me and Kevin had smoked on the path so much the ground beneath the tree was littered with the small marijuana butts. I went to my stash and got out my weed. I rolled a nice fat joint, a skill I had acquired up on the hill with Kevin. We used to see who could roll the most perfect joints. I wasn't as good as Kevin but I was good. Wanda was in the bathroom curling her hair in the mirror when I walked in smoking

## Finding Daddy

the joint. I wish I had a camera to capture the look on her face. "Girl, where you get that from?"

"From Kevin." I wasn't ready to tell Wanda about my stash just yet. "You are full of surprises."

It wasn't long before we were under the spell of the marijuana.

We were in the bathroom singing in the mirror and being goofy. Then we heard the loud screeching of tires and the sound of metal scraping against metal. Wanda and I both were moving toward the bathroom window. At that moment the bathroom wall came crashing in and the front of a car was in our bathroom. We both screamed and ran from the bathroom when we saw a man jump out the car and start running away. I ran to the kitchen, grabbed the phone, and dialed 911.

"911 what's your emergency?"

I was totally out of breath from shock. I couldn't believe a car had come crashing into our house.

"911, hello do you have an emergency?" "A car... just crashed...into our house."

"Is anyone hurt ma'am?"

"I... I...don't know. There was a man in the car...but he got out and ran."

"Okay what's your address?" "1967 Morgan Road."

"Okay ma'am, I will dispatch fire and rescue units along with the police. Do you want to stay on the line?"

"No. I need to check on my sister." I hung up not waiting for the operator to respond.

I went into LaWanda's room where I heard her talking excitedly on the phone about what happened.

"Yes Mama, it's in the bathroom!"

I walked out of her room and back into the bathroom. I definitely didn't want to talk to Mama right now. I knew she was going to be upset. I looked in the car window and didn't see anybody else. I then went out to the front porch to wait for the police. I heard the sirens approaching in the distance. I sat on the porch swing and let the evening air run over my face. The paramedics arrived a few minutes later. They wanted to check LaWanda and I out once they realized there was no one in the car. We told them we were fine, just a little shook up. By the time the police had come, Kevin had walked around from his house with his mother. They couldn't believe a car had run into our house. They used a tow truck to pull the car from the house. The hole that was left once they moved the car was so big. Mama pulled up at the same time as the property owner. She ran up the driveway onto the porch and embraced LaWanda and I. It was the first time I had seen Mama show us affection like that. I think the size of the hole in the house when she pulled up scared her to death. She turned to the property owner and started going off. Everybody tried to calm her down. I thought the police were going to take Mama to jail. They had to bring her down to the end of the driveway.

    The police searched the vehicle and found a driver's license in a wallet. Two of the officers went to go see if they could track down the owner of the car or the driver of the car at the address. Some other officers took statements from LaWanda and I. As they were taking our statements, I heard a call come over the radio reporting that they had a suspect from the address and they were bringing him back over to see if LaWanda or I could I.D. him. When the police cruiser pulled up with the man in the back of the cruiser, an officer called LaWanda and I over and asked us if the man in the back was the man we had seen jump from the car. We both looked at the man in the back and nodded our heads 'yes'. It turned out that the man had been driving drunk when he crashed into the house and ran away to avoid being arrested. After the police took the man away, the property owner came over to talk to us. Mama had finally calmed down. The property owner apologized and offered to pay for us to go to a motel until he could get someone to come over and fix the hole in our house. Mama declined the motel offer. She told the property owner that we would stay at Nana's house, but she did make some kind of deal with the property owner concerning the rent.

    Mama had calmed down, but she was still upset. Mama called Nana and told her what happened. After we gathered a few things, we all headed to Nana's house. I don't know why I didn't get in the car with LaWanda. Mama talked about moving the entire way to Nana's house; that and the fact that she was missing hours at work. We stayed at Nana's house five days and I had a ball. I loved spending time with Nana! We would sit around and talk for hours when I wasn't reading to her. Her friend, Ms. Grace, was a

## Finding Daddy

trip. She always had some gossip to share. When we got back to our house, Mama was still complaining about the accident. She started complaining about the neighborhood on a whole. LaWanda didn't seem to care one way or the other, probably because she was about to graduate and she wouldn't have to worry about meeting new people and new friends. I didn't want to leave the neighborhood and I especially didn't want to leave Glenn Hills. I started walking around the neighborhood looking for houses that were for sale and taking down the phone numbers of the realtors when I wasn't working. Ms. Roberts had jotted down some numbers, too. I really think Mama just wanted to move into her own house. She kept saying how she was tired of renting.

    The entire time I was in Seattle with Kevin and his family I kept thinking about moving again. One thing I knew for sure was if Mama said we were moving, she meant it. I kept wondering where we were going to end up and if I would have to start attending a new school. I was also thinking a lot about my relationship with Kevin. I knew I still cared about him and I felt he still cared about me, but I didn't feel like we were growing together anymore. I was also thinking about the fact that he was supposed to start college in the fall and I knew it was going to be difficult trying to be in a relationship with him in college and me still in high school. Besides, Kevin said he wasn't sure if he was going to stay local for college. That would definitely be an issue. I didn't believe in long-distance relationships and, frankly, I didn't know if I could trust Kevin. He was such a flirt. I refused to end up like LaWanda did with Tyrone. By the time we boarded the plane to return back to Georgia, I think we both knew that our relationship was over as we knew it. I think it was best that we ended it when we did because we were still able to remain friends. I still spent time at his house with his little sister and mom and Kevin and I went out on occasion; we were cool.

    I would've never guessed the reason LaWanda wasn't going away to college this coming fall. I don't think anyone would've guessed. I came in from work one night and I knew something was wrong because Mama's car was in the driveway. She was home and that never was a good sign on a week night. I walked into the living room where Mama was pacing up and down and Wanda was sitting on the couch with tears streaming down her face. As Mama paced, she slapped the backside of her right hand into the palm of her left. "You know I have told you over and over again about these boys and their intentions. Now what are you going to do? You thought you was smarter than me and now you crippled yourself. How you going to college now? How you going to get a good job? You think this boy going to be around? You can't do nothing now but take care of a child and you can't even take care of yourself!

I'm done...done...done." Mama said, walking out the living room right past me without speaking,

Had I heard Mama right? Was LaWanda pregnant? I couldn't believe it. How could this have happened? I stood there staring at LaWanda in disbelief. I watched her shoulders go up and down as she sat on the couch crying. I finally went over and sat down next to her and wrapped my arms around her shoulders. "Everything is going to be alright." Even as I said it, I wasn't sure if I believed it. I knew Mama was going to have a hard time forgiving Wanda for this. She had always talked to us about this type of thing. About getting married before we started bringing kids in the world. I think it was more to do with her relationship with daddy than anything biblical. Whichever it was she stressed it religiously. I think that was the night all of Mama's lessons really started making sense to me. "Does Darren know?" I asked, assuming automatically he was the father. LaWanda nodded her head 'yes.'

"What did he say?" "He was scared." "Scared, why?"

"Because I told him Mama was going to trip out. We're going to his house tomorrow to meet his parents."

"Mama talked to his parents?"

"Yes. She was talking about putting me out. Where am I going to go?" LaWanda said, beginning to cry harder.

"You're out of school now. Why don't you just get your own apartment?"

"I don't have the money for all that. Me and Darren thought about getting our own place when we first found out. We just can't afford it. Not with a baby on the way."

"Why not? With both of you working and the money you saved in the bank, ya'll should be able to manage. How long have

## Finding Daddy

ya'll known?"

"We've known for about two weeks, ever since I went to the base for my last check up. I'm seven weeks. I don't have any more money in the bank. I used it all for graduation and my trip."

I couldn't believe it! How could LaWanda not have any money in the bank? Mama had taken us both to the bank downtown and started accounts for us when daddy had first started sending the support checks. I'd been depositing a little money in my account each time I got paid and a little every time the support check came. I had over $5200 in the bank. I had always assumed LaWanda was depositing money in her account as well. How was she planning on going to college?

"How did you spend all your money? How were you planning to go to college?"

"I wasn't planning on going. I was going to work for a year or two more before I decided if I wanted to go to college or not."

What did she mean decide if she wanted to go to college? Mama had been grooming us for college all our lives it seems. It was at that moment I realized that LaWanda had her own concept on life and hadn't been taking heed to Mama. She wasn't planning to go to college and she had ended up pregnant and broke. My head started hurting; I needed to lie down. I gave LaWanda another hug and told her I loved her and left her sitting on the couch alone. I was really disappointed in my big sister. I would've never thought she wouldn't be going to college, or that she would be pregnant right out of high school. I took a shower and got in my bed and stared at the ceiling like I always did when something was heavy on my mind. I just kept thinking LaWanda is pregnant and broke. I told myself I was never going to let that happen to me. Everything Mama had been telling us over the years finally started making since. Life was serious. I made a mental note to make an appointment at the base for a check-up. I wasn't worried about being pregnant, it was just about time for me to get a check-up. I hadn't been in over six months. I thought about what our daddy would do if he was here, or if Wanda would've even gotten pregnant if he was around. My final thought before I went to sleep was I hope Darren is not like our dad.

\*\*\*\*\*\*

My Uncle Clarence dropped me off at the military base

hospital. I always felt strange when I came here. I would be sitting in the waiting area watching all the military personnel coming in and out. I would be thinking to myself what if one of these men was my daddy? What if he came walking in? Would I know him? I still remembered the way he looked all those years ago when he left. I didn't know if I would recognize him if I saw him today. The waiting area of the hospital had soft seats to sit on and an assortment of military brochures and magazines on tables for you to read as you waited. I remember looking around at all the posters and signs encouraging you to be all you can be by joining the military. I came to hate that phrase and grew a distaste for military men all together later on in life. I think the fact that my dad was military and had abandoned us left me bitter with military men all together.

  The receptionist finally called my name. When I got to the desk she told me she needed to update my information, which I felt was odd. It hadn't been a year since I'd last been here. The receptionist was busy hitting keys on the computer's keyboard when she finally looked up and asked did my sisters and I use the military medical facilities in North Carolina. I shook my head.

  "No. I only have one sister. We both live here."

  The receptionist looked at me, then back at the screen, then back at me. "There's actually three girls listed."

  "Three!" I said, leaning over the counter trying to see the computer screen.

  "Yes ma'am, there is a LaWanda Wilson, Lucinda, I'm assuming is you and then there is Kim Wilson. All listed as the daughters of Sergeant Major Robert Wilson.

  My brain was racing. Who was Kim? I had another sister out there somewhere. My dad had another daughter out there. I wondered if he had abandoned her like he did to us. Once the receptionist convinced me that there had been no mistake made, I started pumping her for information. I remember her passing me a piece of paper and a pen as she gave me addresses and dates. When I finally got all the information she could give me and updated my Information, I went back to my seat and sat staring at the paper. I had another sister out there. I couldn't believe it. I didn't know whether to be sad or happy. I wondered if she was light skinned like LaWanda or dark like me? Did she look like our daddy? One

## Finding Daddy

thing I didn't have to ponder anymore was if he had left her like he had us. The listed address for my sister was the same as my father's and his wife, Denise.

I was in a zone the entire ride back from the base. My Uncle Clarence kept asking me what was wrong. He even asked me if I was pregnant. I showed him the papers I received from the doctor and he finally left me to my thoughts. I had planned on going back to Nana's house with him but after hearing the news about having a sister and getting a current address on my dad, I was just anxious to talk to LaWanda. I asked my uncle to drop me off at home. I was hoping LaWanda was home when I got there. I needed to talk to her and let her know what I had found out. My heart started beating faster when we pulled up to the house and I saw LaWanda's car in the driveway. I hurried from my uncle's truck and into the house calling her name as I entered. She was in her room laying down when I came busting through the door. "Guess what? Guess what?" I said fishing the piece of paper I had with the information on it out of my pocket. "We got a sister," I said excitedly, as I unfolded the paper with the information.

"A sister?" LaWanda said, rolling over on her side and rubbing her eyes. "Yes. Look." I offered her the paper and turned on the lamp on the nightstand.

LaWanda took the piece of paper and sat up. She read it and handed it back to me. "What's that? Who is Kim Wilson?"

"That's our sister." I explained to LaWanda how I had gotten the information at the military base when I went for my check-up. After all these years, we finally had a way to contact daddy and not only that, we had a sister. I didn't care that he had a new wife. I had already accepted the fact that he and Mama were never going to get back together. Although I often dreamed about it, Mama had made it clear over the years she would have nothing to do with daddy. I thought LaWanda was going to be as excited as I was. But LaWanda just rolled back over and told me to shut off her light. "You don't care that we can finally contact daddy?"

"No. Why should I? He hasn't tried to contact us over the years. Why would you even care? He hasn't looked back for us since the day he left!"

I couldn't believe it. LaWanda was acting like Mama. How could she be so cold? This was our daddy. "I'm going to write him. I'm going to send him some pictures of us from your graduation, too. He probably didn't know how to contact us."

"Do what you want. Turn out my light."

My earlier excitement had been reduced to a dark void just that quickly. What if he really didn't want to see us? What if he really didn't love us? I refused to believe that. We were his girls. He had said so himself. I was going to reach out. I was graduating next year and I wanted daddy to be there when I did. At LaWanda's graduation almost the entire graduating class had both parents present. It didn't matter if the parents were still together or not.

That was the one thing that was missing from LaWanda's graduation. Toya's father had even flown in from Dallas to attend her graduation. Toya surprised us all when she came by the house with her dad and announced she was enlisting in the military. Her father was a drill sergeant in the Army. It was so crazy. She had never even talked about her dad before she said he was coming for graduation. I wanted my daddy to show up at my graduation so all my friends could meet him and we could take some pictures. I had high hopes and that's why I was going to make sure I got in contact with daddy. I was going to the post office first chance I got and send him a certified letter.

# CHAPTER 11
## DADDY'S ARMY EXPERIENCE

    The Vietnam jungle surrounded all that entered its heavy foliage. During the conflict between America and Vietnam in the sixties, soldiers would travel through the hot, irriguous boscage in full field gear and carrying an M-16. Fueling up off of meals ready to eat or as they were commonly called, MRE's. The heat was oppressive causing soldiers to sweat so much their fatigues would feel like an extra thick layer of skin. The thick forest above allowed no sun light so one could never tell the time of day except by the humidity, which was almost as bad at night as it was during the day. Soldiers moved in an almost choreographed fashion through the darkened jungle knowing the Viet-Cong could pop up at anytime and launch a deadly attack. Communication in the bush was rarely done verbally between soldiers when they were moving through the bush. They had to be alert and focused. Talking could be a deadly distraction. Robert Wilson moved carefully, keeping close watch on his surroundings for any movement in the bush around him and for booby traps. The Viet-Cong were infamous for setting traps. His unit's mission was to secure a perimeter around Saigon where the North Vietnamese army had started attacking heavily. Robert saw movement through his peripheral on the right and dropped down on his belly and gave the signal for the rest of his unit to take cover. Moments later the jungle erupted with gunfire. Robert's unit returned fire into the bush. Bullets lit up the night and cut down the brush above Robert's head. He crawled into a position of cover behind a huge sapling and put his M-16 on three round burst and began to pepper areas of the jungle where he saw flashes with gunfire.

    The gun battle lasted for seven minutes before the Viet-Cong retreated. In the aftermath, six American soldiers lay dead and four wounded. The Viet-Cong had suffered much larger casualties by the numbers, but the loss of one American soldier was the largest casualty because the entire country felt the lost back home. Robert looked around at the dead and gritted his teeth. He was responsible for these men. He felt like he had let them down. He looked around at the rest of his unit; He saw some soldiers sitting around shell shocked, others were crying and thanking God that they were not among the dead. Then he realized he hadn't let these men down, he had done all he could do in combat which was to keep it together. The same thing he was doing now. After searching the bodies of the three ranking officers among the Viet- Cong, Robert had found some papers containing plans for the Viet- Cong to attack all U.S. Military positions in South Vietnam. When the unit made it to the rally point, there was a general on hand to retrieve the plans Robert had found. He had taken down Robert's name and rank before he boarded a chopper and flew out of camp.

Robert had thought nothing of it. That was over twenty years ago. Today he would meet four star General Lushion Harris again at a ceremony being held to honor veterans. At that ceremony, General Harris would pin a medal of honor to his chest and promote him to Command Sergeant Major. Robert looked at his reflection in the full length mirror. The creases in his uniform pants were razor sharp and his uniform coat fit against his shoulders as if it had been tailored to fit perfectly over his crisp dress shirt. The medals pinned to the left side of his upper chest on his uniform jacket gleamed in the mirror reflecting his many accomplishments. Gail stepped up behind him and wrapped her arms around his waist. Robert smiled as he turned around and placed a kiss on her lips. His hand teased the material of the peach colored camisole she wore causing Gail to squirm and giggle in his arms.

"Stop! How am I going to be able to salute the Sergeant Major later with a straight face and warm skin?" Gail eased from his arms and looked him in the eyes. "I really am proud of you Robert...and I really meant what I said last night."

Robert looked Gail right in her eyes. He really felt like he loved this woman. He had told her just that the night before, as she did him. They had made love with a passion they had never experienced with each other before. They had been seeing each

## Finding Daddy

other for two years. Denise had confronted the both of them on several occasions but she never made a public scene. Denise wasn't a fool. She didn't want the military to launch an investigation into misconduct of an officer and potentially get Robert demoted or dishonorably discharged. She was already complaining about the funds being allocated for LaWanda and

Lucinda. He never heard enough about that: "His dirty little secret," Denise called it. He had finally broke down and admitted that he had gotten Mary pregnant and had even forged documents at the military hospital for one of the births because he wasn't legally married to Mary. Denise had swallowed it all, but not without throwing it back up. She would try to use Kim and her terminally ill daughter to gain leverage in their arguments.

Robert knew that Denise's antics went only but so far; she lived well. He provided for them all and he even paid most of the medical costs for Renee. But Robert was really starting to feel like Gail was the one. Far beyond their sexual relationship, she had a remarkable personality and she was strong and disciplined. Robert loved that about her most. This didn't feel like one of his flings. He had cut everyone else loose with the exception of Denise, but he was beginning to think it was time. He had stayed out all night the night before and he was expected to show up to the ceremony with his wife. He had ignored Denise's pages the night before. Gail had made a nice dinner and they had stayed in making love and celebrating. He had called Denise before he had got in the shower and told her he would be at the house to pick her and Kim up at one. Denise just hung up on him. Now he was holding the woman he loved and about to go home to the woman he was with. "I love you too, baby." Robert kissed Gail once more before picking his keys up off the dresser and heading out of Gail's bedroom.

Gail followed closely on his heels as he made his way to the front door. "I'll see you at the ceremony later, baby. Congratulations. I love you," Gail said from the doorway as Robert unlocked the door to the Jaguar.

"I'll be expecting to see you there in full uniform and I'll get you out of it later," Robert said, as he opened the door.

"Yes sir," Gail said, saluting him from the doorway with a smile.

Robert climbed in the car, started the engine, and backed

out the driveway. He honked his horn before pulling off. Gail stood in the doorway in a dreamy state watching the car head down the street making a right turn at the corner.

Gail went back in the house and filled the tub with bath beads and turned on the water. She walked back in her room and looked in the full length mirror. She placed her hands on her hips and struck a pose. She was feeling so sexy, so free. Robert made her feel like no man had ever made her feel. She knew all about Denise and their marriage, but in her opinion their marriage was over before she had come in the picture. She also knew about Robert's unsavory reputation for being a womanizer but she was sure she had broken his wild streak, especially after last night. She walked over to her dresser and picked up the small velvet box. She opened the lid and gazed at the diamond ring. Robert had proposed to her last night and she had told him, "yes." She never gave a thought to the fact that he was still married to Denise. He had left her long ago, he just had no place to go. He had found his safe haven in her arms and she was never going to let him go. Gail closed the box and placed it back on the dresser.

Gail's only worry with Robert was the two daughters he said he had in Georgia. He claimed Denise kept him from going to see the girls. Gail wanted Robert to have a relationship with the girls. She had grown up without her father. She encouraged Robert to reach out to the girls, but he hadn't done so thus far. That was the one thing that made Gail uneasy about her relationship with Robert.

She was uneasy about the fact that she was sleeping with another woman's husband but she wasn't uneasy about the fact that she may be dishonorably discharged from the military. No, the one thing that made her uneasy was that Robert hadn't put his foot down and made Denise understand the importance his presence would make in the lives of those girls. What woman could be so cold and vindictive toward children of the man they claim to love? He was supportive to her daughter who was ill and he was a big part of their daughter Kim's life and Gail was never going to try and come between that. A girl needed her daddy around. She walked back in the bathroom, turned off the water, and stripped down. She eased her body into the soothing bubbles, closed her eyes, and smiled.

# *CHAPTER 12*
## HEADED TO COLLEGE

    The day of my graduation, I fixed the cap on my head and looked at myself in the mirror. I smiled at my reflection. I had done it! In less than an hour I would be walking across that stage taking my first real step into the real world once they placed that diploma in my hand. This was the one thing in life no one would ever be able to take from me. By this time Mama had gotten approved by the bank and purchased a beautiful Victorian house near Nana. I had made Mama proud. She had taken me to the car lot earlier in the week to look at some cars she said she was going to buy me for graduation. I was happy, but part of me kept thinking she was doing it to make LaWanda feel bad. Mama was still bitter about LaWanda getting pregnant and not going to college. I know Mama loved Crystal, LaWanda's daughter. She had been at the hospital when LaWanda had given birth and she had even taken a week off work when LaWanda brought Crystal home from the hospital. But I knew Mama was disappointed in the fact that LaWanda had gotten pregnant at all and she didn't like Darren either. She let him know it every time he came around. Mama had a way of being disrespectful without actually being disrespectful. She just knew how to change the temperature in a room if that makes any sense.
    Darren was a good father. He always came over and spent time with Crystal. He worked hard and he provided for Crystal as well as LaWanda. Mama just didn't like him. She would always say he was sneaky, probably because he had gotten LaWanda pregnant up under her nose. Rather than Mama admit that LaWanda had made her own decision, she would blame it on Darren. She barely let Darren venture beyond the kitchen when she was home and she sat in the living room watching him like a hawk when he was there. Mama never sat in the living room. She usually stayed in her room talking on the phone or watching T.V.,

throwing back shots of gin on the sly. Whenever she got upset with LaWanda, she would threaten to put her out. A few times she had actually made good on her threats and LaWanda had to go stay with Darren's parents. She always returned and Mama always let her and Crystal come back. I really think Mama did it to try and make LaWanda see she was right and she couldn't make it on her own because she had not followed her blueprint.

    I straightened my gown and walked out to the living room where Mama was waiting with Nana, Uncle Clarence, Janet, Uncle Clyde, LaWanda, and Crystal. They were all smiling as I walked into the living room. I looked at all their faces and felt a wave of happiness sweep over me. Then for a brief second I felt a sense of emptiness. Three very important people were missing: my brother Henry, who was still incarcerated, my Uncle Harvey, who was now strung out on drugs, which none of us could believe. He had always been the rock for the family and the provider, and my dad who I had not heard from since he had left our house all those years ago promising to return. I had sent him a letter with some pictures of LaWanda and I and got no response. That was almost a year ago. I had sent him an invitation to my graduation three weeks ago through certified mail and hadn't received a response. I know he got the invitation for sure. I had even called the number listed on the paper I had with the information on it. I had listened to the woman's voice on the answering machine but I was too chicken to leave a message. I kept hearing the woman's voice over and over again in my head.

    "Hello, you have reached the Wilson residence. We are not able to take your call at this time, but if you would leave a brief message along with your name and number, we will return your call." I wondered if it was the voice of the woman Mama had said called her that time. I wished I had left a message now.

    We piled into the cars and headed to the graduation. I kept thinking that my daddy was going to be at the graduation waiting to surprise me. But he wasn't. I walked across the stage with my head held high and my shoulders straight but inside I felt like crying.

    I made up my mind that day I would not be a failure in life and I wasn't going to look for anyone to be a crutch. I was going to go to college in the fall. I was going to be the first person in my

## Finding Daddy

family to graduate from college with a degree, not for my mother or anyone else, but for me. Mama had bought me a used Toyota Camry and gotten me a job at the nuclear plant she worked at for the summer. I had a lot of fun working at the plant. I worked the first shift. Sometimes Mama would work the same shift as me when she was working over time. Mama had been working in the plant for over seventeen years and was well liked and known by everyone, so naturally everybody treated Mary's daughter with respect. Mama worked in the bio-hazard section of the plant. She was the supervisor of the waste management department of bio-chemicals. I worked as a laborer going back and forth bringing different sized pipes all day to the pipe fitters. I think the pipes were being used by the military for some government nuclear program.

  I had to wear steel toed boots, coveralls, and a hard hat. I also had to wear a device around my neck that monitored the levels of radiation we took in. Sometimes there would be spills in the plant and if you were in an area that had a spill, no matter how small, you would have to be dressed out immediately. The pay was much more than I was receiving working for Woolworth's, but the work was tiring. I remember being so tired from working, I was too exhausted to cash my check at the end of the week. I didn't cash my first check from the job until four weeks after I had started. I walked in the bank with three checks. I mostly slept all weekend when I wasn't going to the library checking on colleges. I wasn't sure where I was going to go to school or what my major was going to be, but I knew I was getting away from Augusta come fall, and this job was going to provide me with some choices and money when I finally made up my mind which school I wanted to go to.

  I remember coming home so tired one Friday night, I fell asleep as soon as I got in. I woke up around four in the morning to get something to drink and saw the mail on the counter. I thumbed through the letters and saw there was a letter from Fort Valley University, it was in a small town about three hours from Augusta. It was one of the Georgia universities I had applied to. I took the letter back in my room and tore it open. I read the letter then I read it again. I had been accepted to the university. I couldn't go back to sleep, I was so excited. I woke LaWanda up and showed her the letter. We both laughed and cried. I had made it! I was going to college. LaWanda was so excited for me she had almost forgotten to tell me her good news. She and Darren had finally found an apartment and were moving in at the end of the week. We both cried some more, but they were tears of joy.

*****

On the day I was leaving for college, I was so nervous. I was supposed to drive myself down to Fort Valley but I had decided to leave my car home. Everything was so close to the campus I didn't need it. Fort Valley was a small town encompassed by peach trees. The town was small and mainly thrived on the college for its livelihood. On the way down to the school me and Mama talked and laughed. We sang songs together and talked about all the accomplishments we had made. Mama had finally managed to get her own house, as an independent, single mother; and I had graduated high school and was on my way into the real world. The closer we got to the town of Fort Valley, I noticed there was nothing but miles and miles of peach trees lining both sides of the back road we were driving on. When we finally pulled up to the campus, my nerves were a wreck. By the time we had left the admissions office, I found out that all the freshmen dorm rooms had been filled and I would be assigned a room in Josie Hall, which was a senior dorm. Mama said I had gotten lucky getting into the senior dorms. We unloaded my things from the car and went in search of Josie Hall. As we walked, I looked at the landscape around the campus. Well manicured lawns and hedges lined the sides of the pathway to Josie Hall. The one thing I did notice right away was that there were a lot of African American students. I never thought so many of us attended college. I always thought any black kid that made it to college was blessed. I was assigned to room 327. When me and Mama entered the room, I could see that it was already occupied by someone else, but the room was empty. Mama helped me organize my things and then began walking around the room. She walked over to the other side of the room and picked up a picture from the desk. "Maybe this is your roommate," Mama said, turning the photo so that I could see it. The girl in the picture was dark skinned and had a bright white smile.

"Mama put that back!" I said, looking at the door hoping

## Finding Daddy

my roommate didn't walk in while Mama was invading her space.

"What! I just want to know who my baby is going to be rooming with."

"Okay Mama, lets go get something to eat."

"Yeah," Mama said, looking at her watch. "I gotta get back to Augusta before my shift."

Mama and I went to one of the town's three restaurants. We had grilled chicken sandwiches and a salad. After we ate lunch, Mama took me back to the campus and we said our goodbyes. I really broke down when Mama got ready to get in the car. I watched her drive away and dried my tears. I went back to my room and began unpacking my clothes and putting them away. When I was done, I laid down on the bed and stared up at the ceiling. The bed wasn't as comfortable as my bed at home, but I'd get use to it. I was really on my own. This was my first step into the real world. I didn't know what to expect, but I was happy I had made it to this stage. I thought about LaWanda and Crystal. I missed my sister and my niece. I missed Mama too and she had been gone less than an hour.

I heard someone putting a key in the lock and then the door opened and the dark skinned girl from the photo Mama had picked up earlier entered. The girl paused in the doorway when she saw me laying on the bed. "Oh I didn't know anyone had moved in. How you doing? Michelle," she said, walking toward my bed and extending her hand.

I quickly sat up on the bed and shook her hand, "Lucinda." "Where did you transfer from?"

I looked at her confused, "I'm from Augusta." "Oh really, what school do they have there?" "I went to Glenn Hills High."

"Is that a university or a community college?" "It's a high school."

Now Michelle looked at me confused. "High school?" Michelle laughed, "I thought you looked a little young. I think you are in the wrong room. This is the dorm for the seniors. The freshmen are over in Thomas and Franklin Halls."

"I know. They told me over at the admissions office that all the freshmen dorms were filled. They assigned me to this dorm." I said, getting off my bed and getting the paper with my room number and assigned hall on it and offered it to her.

~ 155 ~

Michelle took the paper looked it over and handed it back. "That's a first. Well, welcome aboard."

Michelle began to laugh uncontrollably. "What?" I asked. "Girl, you are going to get it. A freshman in the senior's hall.

You are going to be the number one crab," Michelle kept laughing.

I didn't understand what she meant, but I know I didn't like her calling me a crab.

"Crab?!"

Michelle just kept laughing. "Don't get upset freshman. That's what we call all the freshmen. It's just an initiation thing. Don't let it get to you...crab." Michelle said, with a smile. "You'll be alright."

Michelle gave me the skinny on the school and what to expect. She also gave me some good advice that would keep me a step ahead of the other freshmen. The seniors would just sit back and watch freshmen walk around making mistakes, like going the wrong way in the cafeteria. It seemed like the entire campus would be clowning on us. I didn't get it that bad because I lived in the dorm with the upperclassmen and Michelle put me up on a lot of the rules and taught me how to cut corners. She told me to buy used books from the bookstore instead of new ones to save money. She also got me in a work study program, too. It was hard at first because I missed Mama, LaWanda, Crystal, and Nana. I would be up early every Saturday morning trying to get to the phones in the dorm that the students used to call home. Sometimes the line would be so long it would take me over an hour to get a phone. After about two months though, I had really settled in. I met some people from the Augusta area and I was cool with most of the upperclassmen because I lived in the dorm with them.

One of the biggest perks of staying in the senior dorm and having a senior for a roommate was that I was almost always invited to all the parties. Freshmen were never really allowed to attend the parties. Truth be told, most freshmen wouldn't even know there was a party happening. There seemed to be a party everyday in some hall or at someone's house off campus. I fell right into step with the seniors, partying almost every night. I would wake up with hangovers sometimes, struggling to make it to my first class; but by one o'clock when all my classes ended, I

## Finding Daddy

would be ready to party again. I had grown a much stronger tolerance for alcohol. I got so caught up in partying sometimes I wouldn't even make it to class. I hadn't actually chosen a major yet and I was listed as a liberal arts student, a common major for students who weren't sure what they wanted to do yet.

The biggest event on the campus was football. The entire town came out on Saturdays to watch the Wildcats suit up. It was such a big event, all the girls would get their hair done a few days before so they could be looking fly for the game. There was a girl from Atlanta that used to do hair. She would charge anywhere from five dollars up to twenty-five depending on what you wanted. I kept my hair in finger waves and I kept at least ten dollars at all times to get my hair done. We would start tailgating hours before the game eating barbeque and loading up on alcohol and beer. By kick off time, we would be charged up.

It didn't matter if the Wildcats won or lost, we would party hard after the game. I met a lot of guys at the games and during halftime we would wander around and flirt with boys. I had a lot of guy friends, but I really wasn't dating anyone seriously until I started my second semester. I started dating one of the Wildcat football players named Darryl. He was a senior and I had seen him around a few times at some of the parties. Darryl was a linebacker. He stood '6 4" and weighed two hundred and seventy pounds. I always felt safe when we went out, not that there was any potential for trouble. I just felt comfortable that if there was any trouble Darryl would be able to handle it. We would go party hopping on the weekends I stayed on campus. I would go home at least one weekend out of the month. A few of us from Augusta would get together and chip in on the gas and drive back home. Attending school for me was more of an adventure than a learning experience. I started messing up so badly, my GPA had dropped drastically since I had first arrived, but who was going to make me get it together? Mama was back in Augusta and the professors really didn't care one way or the other. They just turned your grades in and let the dean deal with you.

My hair stylist Darlene had invited me to her house for winter break. She lived in Atlanta and I had always wanted to go to the A. I had heard so much about the clubs and parties there and I couldn't wait for winter break. When we first got to Atlanta, we visited her mother then she took me to meet some of her cousins and friends. They were having a big barbeque in her uncle's backyard. There was so much food and so many people it looked like a family reunion. Everybody treated me real nice and I met a lot of men there. Most of the guys were older than me. I was, after all, only nineteen. But I didn't mind, I had always been attracted to older people anyway, male or female. One of Darlene's uncles was really trying to get with me. I think his name was Craig. He had to be in his mid-forties but he dressed and had the mannerisms of the twenty-something guys I was use to dating. We almost hooked up until his wife showed up. It was so funny. She walked up on us while we were sitting at a table talking. She walked up on the table and extended her hand to me, saying,"How are you doing honey, I'm Keiva, Craig's wife."

"Lucinda."

The look on my face must have betrayed my handshake as I took her hand because she quickly snatched her hand back out of mines and turned to Craig.

"So you still chasing these young girls, huh? I hope it fall off dog!"

I felt so uncomfortable after that until Darlene found me sitting at the table by myself. She came over and asked me what was wrong and I told her what had happened; she just started laughing. "Oh, so that's why Keiva was trippin' on Uncle Craig. Girl, don't worry 'bout that. They go through that all the time. You just gotta get to know my folks."

That was the only issue I had my entire stay. I had a ball. I went to so many clubs. It was like everybody knew Darlene. We got into clubs free and I never got asked for I.D. On the night before I was supposed to leave to go back to school, Darlene's aunt had a big card party. I had never seen so many games of spades being played at one time. She had tables set up all around her den. I partnered up with one of Darlene's aunts and we were doing our thing. It seemed like no one could take us off the table. Then an older lady with a blond dye job sat down at the table with her partner. The lady immediately started talking trash. Darlene's aunt matched her word for word. It was hilarious. We were in a tight game. I had been quiet the entire time aside from laughing and sending my bid to my partner. "Your partner too quiet for me, Flo.

## Finding Daddy

All she do is laugh and giggle. I got something to give you the giggles, honey." The lady said, pulling what I thought was an odd looking cigar out of her bag. She lit the cigar and moments later the whole area around our card table smelled like marijuana. The woman took two pulls off the cigar and offered it to me. "Here, honey, hit this and take it slow. You look like a virgin. By the way, my name is Shirley. Dear, folks ain't got no manners. We been sitting here all this time and I don't even know your name."

"Lucinda," I said smiling, and taking the cigar she was offering. I pulled on the cigar like I was hitting a joint and nothing could prepare me for the uncontrollable coughing that would follow. I was coughing so hard I had to push my chair back from the table. I hung my head between my legs and coughed and coughed. Saliva ran down my chin and cheek. I dropped the cigar on the card table and I felt someone patting me on my back real hard.

"You alright, baby?"

I nodded my head yes even though I wasn't. I could hear other people laughing and gathering around the table. I looked up to see who was patting me on my back and was surprised to see Shirley standing over me. Darlene was on my right side asking if I was alright. I kept nodding my head and I was starting to get a hold of myself. "What was that?" I asked.

"That, my dear is that Ganja," Shirley said, reaching over to give Darlene a high five. She picked the cigar up off the card table and lit it back up. She took two deep pulls before she passed the cigar to Darlene.

We resumed our game and even though I hadn't hit the cigar again, I started getting that free feeling I always got when I smoked. By the time the hand was over I was feeling real good. I started talking trash right along with Shirley. In the wee hours of the morning when mostly everybody had left, we were still sitting around smoking and talking trash. I finally started hitting the blunt (that's what they called the cigar with the weed in it), where I was able to smoke without coughing. Shirley stood up and proposed a toast to new friends, long life, and me accomplishing all I wanted in life. I was surprised that she had added me to her toast. Before Darlene and I left, Shirley pulled me to the side and handed me a sandwich bag full of marijuana and her phone number. She told me to make sure I stay in touch with her and I was welcome back to the 'A' anytime. I didn't know it at the time, but this woman would be instrumental in my development into womanhood. The next day I returned to college and continued with my regular routine of partying and hanging out with Michelle and our crew.

One Saturday, Michelle was as excited as I had ever seen her. She said there was going to be a big step show after the game. I really didn't know what to expect. There were students from other schools and groups of step teams. Everybody seemed to be representing some type of organization. One group in particular interested me. The Greek step team was amazing as they walked around with their canes and colorful jackets sporting their insignias. When they took the stage, it was surreal. I felt like I was an extra in *Skool Daze*. They jammed on stage and then did an encore routine as they left the stage and came through the crowd. I was so in awe of their performance, I started asking questions about how to join the organization. I didn't want to be on the step team, but I did want to belong to the group. As a freshman with my suffering grades, that should've been the last thing I was thinking about. But I started going to the library researching all the information I could on the organization. I would try to meet people from the organization at parties and try and forge relationships with them. I wanted in badly.

I had started partying harder and harder and my grades kept slipping further and further. By the end of my third semester, my grades had slipped so bad that I received a letter from the dean informing me that if I didn't raise my GPA next semester I would have to take a semester off. I was shocked. I couldn't believe it. I couldn't get kicked out of school. Mama would have a fit. I had to get focused. I started joining study groups and stopped partying. I even broke up with Darryl. I really didn't have time for a relationship anymore. Michelle helped me as much as she could, but she really wasn't a good influence. Her grades weren't in trouble and she loved to party. My help came from an unexpected source. I was in my dorm room rolling the last bit of the Ganja Shirley had given me, when I remembered I had her number. I finished rolling the blunt, a practice I had learned the night I had stayed out with Shirley and Darlene; a practice that made me popular on campus. When I returned with the Ganja and started

# Finding Daddy

rolling blunts, the whole campus started doing it. I walked to the phone booths located on the first floor of the dorm and saw they were empty. People rarely made calls to loved ones during the week. I picked up a phone and dialed the number on the piece of paper. The phone was picked up on the third ring. "Hello."

I heard a lot of noise and music in the background and I paused before I spoke. I didn't want to start talking to an answering machine. "Hello," I said, somewhat timidly.

"Hello, who is this?" "Hello...is Shirley there?"

"This is she, who am I speaking with?"

"Hey, this is Lucinda. I don't know if you remem…"

"Oh hey, dear. How you been? What took you so long to call?" Shirley said cutting me off.

I paused again before speaking."I'm alright...how have you been?"

"I been good, dear. So when you coming for another visit?"

"I don't know."

"Why, you didn't like our company?" "No, no I had a great time. It's not that." "Well, what's wrong, honey, you alright?"

It was something in her voice that made me feel the need to tell her everything that was going on. When I was done explaining to her about the letter from the dean, she told me not to worry and that she would help me. Over the next few weeks I talked to Shirley on the phone everyday into the wee hours of the morning. She helped me with my studies and had even helped me write a paper for my sociology class. She talked to me about so many things. Whenever I got off the phone with her I would return to my room and lay in my bed thinking about the things she told me for hours. She would often be around her boyfriend Tim when we were on the phone. She would be talking to him sometimes in the midst of our conversations on the phone. I would meet Tim sometime later and realize he was the source of the Ganja Shirley had given me. I ended up going to Atlanta and staying with her for a while later on and met some very interesting people. They dealt with a lot of upper echelon clientele: doctors, lawyers, and businessmen. I dated a few of these men and experienced some really nice times. Shirley kept encouraging me to transfer schools.

At the end of the fourth semester I had brought my grades up just enough to be able to attend next semester. I went out that weekend and partied so hard that I was throwing up all day Sunday. As I was on my knees hugging the toilet, I made a tough decision. A decision that probably saved my college career and really let me know I was ready to be responsible in this world. I had to transfer schools. I started applying to different universities the next day.

*****

Shirley invited me to come stay with her during summer break. I arrived in Atlanta on a Friday afternoon. Shirley and Tim met me at the airport. The first thing I noticed about Tim was that he was much younger than Shirley. He wasn't as young as me, but I knew he was in his early or mid twenties. He had a caramel complexion with a curly afro and he spoke with an accent like he was from one of the islands. I expected my time with Shirley was going to be full of adventure, but I was wrong. We did have some fun times. We all went to Six Flags and we went camping in the mountains. But most of the time Shirley was schooling me on the do's and don'ts of the real world and took me around applying to schools. We finally settled on Voorhees University in South Carolina. I say *we* because Shirley was the one who found the school, drove me to South Carolina and to the college campus. She had become like an older sister to me. I told her everything and I always felt she was honest with me. I found comfort in her and the relationship we had. By the time vacation was over, I had matured more than I would've imagined for myself. I had also been accepted to Voorhees. I had curved my appetite for partying. Instead I craved success.

When fall arrived, I started attending Voorhees as a criminal law major. I knew immediately Voorhees was nothing like Fort Valley. First of all, the town was a lot smaller and so was the population. The college campus was made up of old buildings which looked liked they hadn't been touched since they were built. The campus offered no real landscape other than the education buildings and the student dorms. Honestly, I called Shirley several times a day my first couple of days. I didn't think I was going to make it. The dormitories were the worse. The rooms were a lot smaller and offered very little space for two people to really live together comfortably. The showers were so filthy and there was mold growing in some of them. I eventually started going off campus all together to use the bathroom and take care of my

# Finding Daddy

personal hygiene.

I had to have my car. There was virtually nothing in the town but the general store, the college, and the people. The people were strange to me, too. Most of the students were from small towns in Georgia I had never heard of or other places I hadn't heard of in other states. The university wasn't popular at all, which was one of the reasons Shirley insisted that's where I needed to be. Most of the students there wore outdated clothes and were weird to me. The school didn't even have a football team. They played basketball for homecoming. I was sick.

There were a few people I knew from Augusta there. I would hang out with them from time to time, but I never partied unless we went home for the weekend. The two small hole-in-the-wall bars they had in the town didn't look attractive enough from the outside, so I never ventured inside. My roommate was from a small town not too far from the school. We didn't hang out much, but she was cool. Sometimes we would go to Orangeburg, South Carolina to the mall. It was the only place to go unless you drove to Augusta. There really were no activities to distract the students from learning. My first semester there was so boring, I picked up twenty one hours worth of classes at Voorhees and three extra hours at the Demark campus my second semester just to keep from being bored. I was doing really well. I had brought my GPA back up to a 3.5. I started attending the meetings of different campus organizations and getting involved in as many campus activities as I could find. I ran for homecoming queen and I was Miss Pan Hellenic and Miss Delta Sigma Theta. By my second year, I was starting my internship.

I did my internship at a maximum security state correctional facility. That was a very interesting experience. During my internship, I realized most of the men incarcerated at the prison grew up suffering the same upbringing as myself in the sense that most of these men grew up in single parent households without a father. I empathized with them. I thought about Henry and his stint in prison. I had received a letter from Henry recently telling me he had gotten in contact with his biological father and they were writing each other. Working in the prison made me think about my daddy because most the men I counseled talked about not having any positive male role models in their lives. It made me want to find my daddy and tell him all that was on my heart. Most of the men I spoke with in the prison said they would love to contact their fathers even if it was just to ask them why they hadn't been there for them. There was one particular inmate that made me get back on my search for my daddy. His name was Jerod Robinson and he had been trying to get in contact with his son for six months. He came into my office one day excited because he had recieved a letter from his fifteen year old son. He read the letter to me and when he was finished he broke down and started crying. He was so happy he had been able to get in contact with his son, but more than anything he was happy his son had forgiven him. His son had said something so prolific, in the letter his son had written. I never forgot it. He said, "Your behavior as a father in my life has been unacceptable, but understandable."

    I left the prison that day and returned to my dorm. I immediately began to look for the paper I had put away with daddy's information on it. I had never thrown the paper away and I made sure I updated my information at the military hospital every six months to keep tabs on daddy. I had gotten the nerve to call the number on the paper. When I did, I spoke to a woman who was probably daddy's wife. When I told her who I was, she said my daddy didn't have any daughters besides hers and hung up. I was heartbroken and I never called back. But after that day at the prison with Jerod, I felt a new motivation. I went to the phones and dialed the number. A woman's voice picked up on the second ring.

    "Hello."

    It was the same woman's voice I heard last time I called. I started to hang up the phone. My heart was beating so fast and then it just came out. "Hello, may I speak with Kim, please?"

    "May I ask who's calling?"

    "Yes. Ms. Robinson from the Department of Labor." "Is there a problem?"

    "No ma'am, I just need to make sure all her information is correct in our system before we update it." I couldn't believe how easy it was for me to lie.

    There was a pause then I heard what sounded like papers being shuffled, "Well, Kim is not in right now. She's at work but I can give you the number to her job if you really need to speak with her."

## Finding Daddy

"I would appreciate that. The quicker we update the information, the better."

"Okay. She works at Red Barren and the number is 585-7065." I almost screamed. I couldn't believe I had pulled it off. "Thank you very much, ma'am. Have a nice evening." I hung up before she could respond. I quickly dialed the number she gave me adding the area code. "Red Barren, would you like to place an order for pick up or delivery?"

I was nervous again but I wasn't going to blow it now. "Umm, may I speak to Kim please?"

"Hold on," the female voice on the other line said. "Kim!"

I heard a lot of noise in the background while I waited. Then I finally heard someone picking up the phone. "Hello."

Was this really her? What should I say? I got my nerves in order as much as I could and I wished I had smoked some Ganja before I called, but I hadn't smoked weed in almost two years. I swallowed hard.

"Hello Kim?" "Yes, who is this?" "Kim Wilson?" "Yes. Who is this!"

"My name is Lucinda Wilson and I am your sister."

There was a long pause. "Hello, hello."

"How did you get this number?"

"Your mother gave it to me. Did you hear what I said? We are sisters. Robert Wilson is my daddy, too."

There was that long pause again, so I just went on to explain how I had been looking for daddy for all these years and how he had left LaWanda and I. As I was speaking, I could tell that this wasn't the first time Kim had heard about LaWanda and I. When I was done speaking, I expected her to have a million questions, but there was that silence again. I knew she was still on the line because I still could hear noise in the background. "Hello, did you hear me?"

"Yes, I heard you. I just lost my sister. I am at work and I can't deal with this right now…it's too much," Kim said, before hanging up on me.

I stared at the phone in disbelief. Had she said her sister had just died? Was there another sister? No, it couldn't be or she would've been listed on the records at the hospital. I couldn't believe it. I thought she would be happy to learn she had a sister. I

~ 165 ~

hung up the phone and went back to my room. I was so disappointed. I lay across my bed and began to cry. Was I ever going to find my daddy?

I fell back into my life at school and tried to forget about the phone conversation I had with Kim. I told myself I wasn't going to bother looking for my daddy anymore. I took a job in the school cafeteria as a food service administrator. I was in charge of the payroll and organizing the food that would be prepared throughout the week. It was a cool job. My supervisor was an older man named Ronald. He was so cool and understanding, I thought of him as a father figure. The other employees thought there was something going on between us, but it was strictly platonic. I think people were just jealous of my position and the relationship I had with Ronald, but I didn't care. The truth of the matter is I hadn't dated much at all since I had come to Voorhees. I had been so focused on trying to get back on track from my activities at Fort Valley, I really didn't think about dating. I really wasn't that interested in anyone. Well, there was one person, but there was a big conflict with that because he was a professor at the university. I had been hawking him since I arrived. His name was Frank Owens and he was a handsome, dark skinned man in his mid forties. For some reason I noticed myself always attracted to people older than myself. He knew I was feeling him; and I knew he was feeling me, too. I could tell by the way he looked at me. He had even pulled me aside one day on campus and spoke to me about a grade I had gotten and before he walked away he said, "You know students and teachers can't fraternize, it would be inappropriate."

I started to become more aggressive with Frank after my internship ended and he reluctantly gave into me and we began creeping. A few people on campus suspected something was going on but no one knew for sure. Frank lived in a town about forty minutes away from the university so we would spend a lot of time at his house. I started spending so much time off campus that I decided to just move off campus all together. My roommate told me about a man trying to rent a double wide trailer on the outskirts of town. I checked it out and the man renting the property looked like he was around seventy years old. He was real nice. Once I moved into the trailer, he would come over to check on me and make sure everything was alright. If anything needed to be fixed in

## Finding Daddy

the trailer, he would come fix it free of charge. Sometimes I would cook dinner for him and we would sit around and talk for hours.

He told me about his daughter and grand kids who lived in New York. He used to say I reminded him of his daughter and that made me feel good. The only problem I had living in the trailer was that when it would rain, the roof sounded like it was going to cave in, other than that I loved it. I stayed in that trailer until I graduated from school.

I continued to see Frank until two weeks before I graduated. I knew that I was about to move into another stage in my life and I knew that Frank and I were not going where I was headed, so I broke it off. I still had that part of me that refused to be hurt. After graduation, I returned back to Atlanta for a while and took a job as a paralegal. I loved my job and I finally felt like I was fully coming into my own. I had my own apartment, I bought a Honda Accord, and I started taking a real estate class in the evenings. I even started going back to church every Sunday. It felt so good to be back in the church. I hadn't been in so long. I felt the need to go and give praise to God for all the things he was blessing me with. I attended Hopewell Baptist church in Norcross, Georgia. I met a lot of good people in that church and I felt our congregation was strong and I loved the fellowship worship.

On December 31, 1996 the church was having a New Year's service. I was supposed to be meeting friends there but when I got there, the church was so crowded I couldn't find my friends. The service would be starting soon so I found a pew that wasn't filled up and took a seat on the end near the aisle. I kept looking over my shoulder at the door to see if I saw my friends. I saw an attractive light skinned man come from the back of the church and began walking toward me. For some reason I didn't look away and neither did he. He moved well in his three piece gray suit. He wore a blood red tie and matching gators. His attire was nice, but it was those eyes that smiled. I almost felt like a deer in the headlights. His hand brushed my hand as it rested on the edge of the pew and as he passed, our fingers locked. I just stood up and introduced myself, which was surprising to me. At the time I was single and really not looking for a relationship or even dating and I never approached men; they always pursued me. Since my relationship with Frank, I had become committed to myself and my new growth. I had a degree and a job actually working in my field after graduating, which wasn't always the case with college graduates.

"Hello, Lucinda. My name is Derick Gibbs. Do you normally worship here or did you just come for the New Year's celebration?"

"Yes, I worship here. I'm here every Sunday at seven a.m. I've been coming here for a while. You're definitely a new face. Happy New Year, praise God," I said, surprised at how I was warming up to this man, and he was clearly warming up to me; he hadn't let my hand go.

"Thank you. Happy New Year to you as well. I attend the ten o'clock service on Sundays. I guess that's why we've been missing each other. Why don't you get here a little late this Sunday?" Derick said with a smile, finally releasing my hand.

I smiled back. "Why don't you get up early?"

"Why don't you let me get your digits and I'll call you and we can figure out how we are going to do this cause I gotta see you again, whether it's in the house of the Lord or my house for some real down home Louisiana shrimp gumbo."

"Where you going to get some down home Louisiana shrimp gumbo from in Georgia?" I asked, wondering if I should give Derick my number. I sure wanted to. The cologne he was wearing was intoxicating.

"My aunt is in town from Louisiana. She made it today, honest. You can come over after the service and eat with us."

I smiled again. He was smooth and I liked him, but no way was I going to his house after service tonight. "462-0901. Get the recipe from your aunt and you can make it for me at my house sometime, but not tonight."

"Are you here with someone? Can we sit together?"

"Of course," I said, sitting back down and sliding inside the pew allowing Derick to sit down. We sat together in that pew the entire service whispering like little kids in Sunday school. I felt like I had known him for so long. He was exactly what I had prayed for; tall, educated, and God fearing. Nana always said the best man was the man that loved God more than he loved you and I got that vibe from this man as we talked in hushed tones. He didn't have any kids because he didn't want to be a father out of wedlock.

## Finding Daddy

He was brought up with a strong Baptist rearing. I couldn't ignore the fact we had met on New Year's Eve at church. Service ended at eight and Derick walked me to my car after the parking lot cleared out. We were so busy saying goodbye and talking, we didn't realize we were the last two in the lot until the Reverend got in his Cadillac and pulled out of the lot. Derick promised to call the next day.

When I got home, I called Mama and told her about meeting Derick at the church, but I think she was a little tipsy so I just wished her a Happy New Year and got off the phone. I knew this man had me excited when I realized I had been home for forty-five minutes and was still walking around in my heels. I finally took the heels off and ran a hot bubble bath. I sat in the water trying to relax, but I couldn't get Derick out of my head. When I got out the tub, I turned on the T.V. and watched the New Year's Eve countdown with Dick Clark. I had never been able to stay awake until the ball dropped, but that night I watched the ball drop, then I got on my knees and thanked God for answering my prayers before going to sleep.,

Derick and I begin to see a lot of each other. Whenever we were not working, we were together. He even started attending the seven A.M. Sunday morning service at church. We did so many things together but the most important thing to me was our communication. We talked about everything and I always felt so comfortable. I stopped calling Mama and LaWanda as much, as I was truly coming into my own. I was in love. Derick and I had planned to go away for Christmas. We were going to rent a nice cabin in North Georgia and we were going to prepare Christmas dinner and just have a good time. I had completed my classes in real estate and had my license. I was working at the law firm still, but I was also an active real estate agent. I made a nice piece of money selling homes. I was thinking about going at it full time, but I was still holding out for the firm I was working for. The good thing about being an agent was when there were cancellations on time shares or properties like the cabin resort in North Georgia that the realty company I was working for at the time managed, they would offer the rental or time share at an even lower discounted rate than we already received. I took full advantage whenever I could. Derick and I traveled all over. The realty company I worked for managed properties all over the country and people were always canceling time shares.

December 25th was cool and clear. We were sitting at the dinner table eating when Derick jumped up suddenly and ran in the bedroom of the cabin. He returned with a single long stemmed rose with a card taped to it and handed it to me. I peeled the small card away from the rose and read it. It was Proverbs 18:22. When I looked up from the card, Derick was holding a velvet box with a ring in it. "Will you marry me?"

I was so happy. I was at a loss for words. I mean, I really couldn't speak. I laughed for twenty minutes, no exaggeration.

I know Derick thought I was crazy. I finally got myself together and said, "yes." The first person I called was Mama. She was happy for me. She liked Derick. I think it was because he was light skinned. We set the date for August of the next year. It was like

God was really shining in me. I was doing so well with the realty company, I quit working for the law firm all together. Derick and I bought our first home together three months before we were married. Our wedding was held at the church where we first met. Mr. Robinson, a long-time family friend, walked me down the aisle and gave me away. He was the perfect stand-in for my daddy, who I hadn't really tried to contact in years since I talked to my sister Kim that time when she was at work. The ceremony was beautiful. Three of my bridesmaids wore crimson and three wore cream. The flower girl tossed rose petals as she made her way down the aisle. We wrote our own vows and had a 70's themed reception.

The blessings kept on coming. We found out I was pregnant a year after we were married and Derick received a promotion at his job. With a baby coming, we decided we needed a bigger house so we put our house up for sale and began looking for a new one. We moved into our new house a week before I gave birth to Derick Jr. Derick was so happy. I had given him a son. I was happy to be a mother. Nana said I was a natural at it. I was so attentive and careful with Derick Jr. He was his father's son, but he was my baby. Derick and I were truly happy and God was shining on us. But something inside me didn't feel complete. I didn't know

## Finding Daddy

what it was until Father's Day came around. Me, Derick, and Derick Jr. went to a nice restaurant to celebrate and as I watched Derick with our son, it hit me why I didn't feel complete. I broke down right there in the restaurant and we left before our meal came. Derick didn't complain one time on the way home. He just kept asking me what was wrong. When we got home, I got Derick Jr. ready for bed and went and got in the shower. When I got out, I walked in our bedroom and Derick took me in his arms. I felt so safe and warm there that I just broke down again. I told Derick everything I was feeling about not having my father in my life. I told Derick our dad hadn't been in mine or LaWanda's life, but I never told him the effect it had on me. I had ruined his Father's Day because I couldn't be with my daddy. This would become a pattern that I would continue to trace for a long time. It got worse every year.

  By the time our second son Daniel was born, we had moved yet again to a larger house on the outskirts of Atlanta. Derick's job had transferred him to the Atlanta area office. I was still selling real estate, but I had also taken a job working for the airline and I loved it. The pay was decent, but what I really loved was the benefit of being able to fly for free. Derick and I would constantly go on trips with the kids, flying to different locations. During these times, Derick would always encourage me to try and find my daddy. He had even helped me get a new current address for daddy. Since I hadn't been to the military base hospital anymore, I wasn't sure if the information I had was good. I know the phone numbers I had were no longer good. Kim didn't work at the restaurant anymore and the home number had been changed. Derick always suggested that we just drive to Raleigh and try and find daddy. At times, I think he wanted to find my daddy more than I did. He would just come to me with stories that he had read or heard about people being reunited with their parents after years. I wanted to find my daddy and find that connection I was missing, but I think fear of rejection reared its ugly head again and would never let me get up the nerve to get in the car and just drive to Raleigh.

## CHAPTER 13
### IT'S FINALLY DONE

Gail looked out the kitchen window at Robert and Kim in the driveway. That girl sure looked like her daddy, Gail thought to herself. She wished she had established a better relationship with Kim over the years, but it really wasn't her fault. She had tried to develop a relationship with Kim early on when Robert had first left Denise, but Kim hadn't budged; she had sided with her mother against Gail. Whenever we all went out somewhere, Kim always acted cold and standoffish. This had been going on for the last twelve years. Gail looked down at the ring on her finger; a nice one karat pear shaped diamond set nicely in platinum. It was a different ring than the one he had first given her thirteen years earlier, but it held the same promise. Robert still hadn't given her the dream wedding they had talked about. He had retired from the military and was receiving full benefits. Denise was being difficult in giving Robert a divorce. She was holding something over his head and Gail believed it had something to do with Robert's other two daughters. Whatever it was, Robert didn't want it to come out.

Denise had been dragging this divorce out for years. She would always agree to sign the divorce papers and then renege at the last minute coming up with some excuse. Then Robert wouldn't hear from her or see her for months. He had given her the house and two cars but Denise wanted everything Robert had. She had the attitude that everything Robert had, she was responsible for. Gail understood Robert not wanting to give Denise any type of control or joint control of any of his properties, homes, or cars, but Gail didn't understand why Robert wouldn't go to court. He had earned his way in the world dedicating his life to this country. He was an honored serviceman. Surely any judge would see that. She was sure no judge would make Robert give up half his assets to Denise.

He had already given her more than enough. Gail knew it was something holding Robert back from pressing the issue into court. They had even gone to a lawyer for a consultation and he assured Robert that if he took the case, he would protect all his assets. But Robert went no further than paying the lawyer a retainer, keeping the attorney on stand by just in case. That's why Gail knew it was something Denise was holding over her man's head and she was almost sure it had something to do with Robert's other two daughters.

Gail had heard arguments between Denise and Robert on the phone over money and "those girls," as Denise called them. Every time Gail asked Robert why he didn't get in contact with his other daughters, he would get a sad look in his eyes and just shrug his shoulders and say, "it's complicated." After a while Gail just stopped pressing the issue. Gail turned the faucet on and filled the sink with warm dish water. She saw Kim wiping at her eyes as she handed Robert a piece of paper. Robert took her in his arms and held her. Gail felt her nose begin to tingle and her eyes began to burn with tears. She rubbed her right index finger under her right eyelid and turned off the faucet. She watched Kim walk back to her car crying. Robert started back up the driveway toward the house. He no longer moved with the swagger he once had, suffering two strokes in the last four years. Gail hadn't left his side since the first one. She retired from the military five years shy of her planned enlistment and dedicated all her time to taking care of Robert. Gail wiped her hands on her apron and went to meet Robert at the door. When he walked in, he took her in his arms and kissed her. "It's finally done," he said. Robert handed her the piece of paper.

Gail took the piece of paper and read it. She smiled as she led Robert into the living room and got him seated in his chair. She folded the piece of paper and slipped it in the pocket on her apron. "I'll go make you a cup of coffee."

"Thank you, baby. I love you."

"I love you more," Gail said as she walked back toward the kitchen. She began to hum an old church hymn. Denise had finally signed the papers the attorney had drawn up for the divorce on the terms of a mutual agreement. Gail looked at the ring on her finger again, and thought, valued against the piece of paper in her pocket, it didn't have the value of a nickel gumball machine ring.

# CHAPTER 14
## DADDY AND DAUGHTER CONNECTION

My trip to Raleigh was supposed to be strictly business. I was there to attend a weekend seminar on motivational speaking. I flew in Friday morning and called my friend Ms. Eunice. I met her in Kennedy airport two years earlier when one of our flights had been unexpectedly delayed. We met in the airport coffee shop. She had walked up to the table I was sitting at and smiled. "You have good energy."

I returned her smile. "Thank you," I said. I expected her to go on about her business but she kept standing there. She finally asked if she could sit down with me. I didn't know this lady from Adam, but I didn't get a bad vibe from her so I invited her to sit with me. We sat in that coffee shop for five hours talking. It was like we had an instant connection. She told me that I should get into motivational speaking because I gave off great energy and I could inspire so many people. I was flattered, but I wasn't sure about the motivational speaking. She encouraged me to take a Toastmasters course to help me get comfortable with speaking. Before I reported back to the plane for the flight, we exchanged information and stayed in contact. I had followed her advice and took the Toastmasters course and did some small speaking engagements locally for the church. I was excited about attending the convention.

I called Ms. Eunice as soon as I got settled in the hotel. We met for lunch and did a little shopping afterward. Then we went back to the hotel to get dressed for the introduction ceremony in the hotel's banquet room. I met so many people and collected so many business cards. It felt good to be connecting. When I got back to my room, my feet were killing me from walking around in heels for all those hours. I took a shower and called Derick. "Hey baby."

"Hey love, how is everything? Did you get booked in the hotel all right? I was about to put an APB out on you. I haven't heard from you since you left yesterday morning." Derick said chuckling.

I looked over at the clock on the night stand and saw it was after twelve. I didn't notice the introduction ceremony had lasted so long, no wonder my feet were killing me. "I'm sorry baby. I had lunch with Ms. Eunice earlier and then we went to the introduction ceremony. How's everything at home?"

"Everything's fine. The kid's haven't died from starvation if that's what you mean," Derick said laughing.

I laughed. "What are they doing?"

"Derick is playing a video game and Daniel is asleep. Do you think you are going to have time to go by the address we got for your father?"

I hadn't really thought about it. I always carried the address with me on a just-in-case basis and here I was. "I...I really didn't think about it."

"I think you should at least check it out. You're right there. You got nothing to lose and everything to gain. Please baby, think about it."

"I will."

"Okay baby. Call me in the morning when you wake up so you can talk to the boys before they go to their football games. I love you."

"I will. I love you more. I will speak with you in the morning." After I got off the phone with Derick, I went to my pocketbook and took out my wallet. I pulled out the piece of paper with the address on it from behind my social security card and stared at the address. Derick was right. I couldn't be this close to my daddy and not attempt to go and see him. We had to meet the group for a meeting tomorrow at one o'clock, and then we were free until seven thirty tomorrow evening. I would ask Ms. Eunice if she knew how far we were from the address. I knew she said she had family in the area. Maybe they could tell us where the address was. I tried to get some sleep but I couldn't. Thinking about the possibilities kept me tossing and turning all night.

## Finding Daddy

The next morning, Ms. Eunice and I met for breakfast and I began to tell her about my father and my search. By the time I finished, she was on my side of the booth we were sitting in holding me in her arms. I had tears streaming down my face staining my blouse. She asked me to let her see the address. I pulled out the paper and handed it to her. She looked at the paper and began to smile. "I know exactly where this is. I have a cousin who lives in Fayetteville not too far from this street. We can probably drive there in about forty five minutes, no more than an hour. We can drive out there after our meeting."

The meeting ended around 2:30. I was so nervous when we got in the rental car after the meeting. I had that feeling I used to get when I was younger and knew I was in trouble. I started thinking about the day daddy left and promised to come back and never did. What if he didn't want to see me? What if he didn't remember me? Ms. Eunice turned down a street with neatly manicured lawns and huge Victorian homes that were almost all built in an identical manner barring color. I looked for the address written on the paper. It was coming up on the right side. Ms. Eunice slowed down. I saw the name **WILSON** written on the mailbox. My palms were sweating so badly that the paper I was holding was moist. My heart was beating so fast I thought I was going to need an asthma pump. There was a car underneath the carport but it was covered up. I got out of the car and walked up the path leading to the front door. I pressed the bell and waited. I heard no movement coming from inside the house. Ms. Eunice got out of the car and started up the driveway. "Knock on the door, honey, the doorbell may not work."

I knocked on the door softly. I still heard no movement. I tapped on the door again a little harder this time. I felt the pits of my arms begin to perspire. I felt nervous and anxious all at the same time. After about two minutes, Ms. Eunice suggested we leave a note. We knew this was the house. His name was right there on the mailbox. I was so discouraged I just got back in the car and told her I was ready to leave. Ms. Eunice tried to comfort me on the ride back, but I just felt defeated. I refused to cry though. I wasn't going to allow that hurt back in my life. I was happy. I might not have felt whole but I was happy. I had Derick and my boys. Ms. Eunice promised we would come back the next day but I really didn't want to. We attended the dinner that evening and ironically the keynote speaker touched on rebuilding relationships that had failed to reshape life. I thought about his words all night. I even told Derick the things he had said and how I felt like he was talking directly to me. Derick encouraged me to go back the next day. He said it was a divine power at work bigger than my emotions.

The next day Ms. Eunice and I had breakfast and immediately left for Fayetteville. Ms. Eunice kept telling me to pray and think positive. She told me to keep faith with God. We said The Serenity Prayer together and I continued to pray. When we turned on the street we had been on the day before, I immediately noticed there was a white Jaguar under the carport. I wasn't sure if dad still drove or what kind of car he drove if he did, but my heart started beating faster. Ms. Eunice parked and I said another prayer before I opened the door and got out of the car. I walked up the path and knocked on the door. I listened but I heard no movement from inside. I knocked again, and again. Still nothing. I looked back toward the car where Ms. Eunice was. I was starting to feel worse than I had yesterday. That's when I noticed Ms. Eunice pointing at the side of the house. I walked to the side of the walkway near the carport and saw a man in a Hawaiian shirt and beige khakis coming out of a side door. He had a head full of gray hair and a hump on his back. He moved pretty slowly but without assistance. When he looked up and I saw his eyes, I knew this man was my daddy. He and LaWanda had the same eyes. I almost broke down right there, but I held it together.

"May I help you, young lady?" Daddy asked, as I approached.

I couldn't believe it. This was my daddy. "How are you doing?" "Oh, I'm alright for an old man."

"Do you know who I am?"

"No baby, I don't think I know you. Are you looking for Gail?" I was hurt that he didn't recognize me. I wanted to cry but I didn't. We were standing near the car that was covered up. I took this frail man's hands into mine and held them. "Look at me" I said, "I'm Lucinda."

Daddy immediately grabbed a hold of me and hugged me. I felt his frail body against mine. It felt like his body had

## Finding Daddy

straightened up a little bit. I could tell he was sick, but it felt like God was transferring life from me back into the source from which it came. We both stood there holding each other and crying. Ms. Eunice got out of the car and came up the walkway. I introduced her to daddy. She told him how we had come the day before and how I was disappointed when no one was here. She teased me a bit, saying she bet I was happy I came back. Daddy invited us in the house and introduced us to Ms. Gail. She was so nice and she seemed genuinely happy to meet me. She fried us some chicken and we all just sat around talking. I had so much to catch daddy up on. I forgot about all the questions I told myself I would ask him once we met. But those questions didn't seem important right now. I wanted to tell him about his grand kids, about Derick, about all the things LaWanda and I had done.

  We didn't leave until after nine that night. God had answered my prayers after what seemed like a lifetime. I felt reborn. Daddy promised to come by the hotel the next day before my flight left.

  We attended the last leg of the convention but we arrived late. Before the speaker closed the meeting he asked if anyone had anything they wanted to share. Ms. Eunice got up and went to the microphone and told everyone about the experience she just had with me and my dad. She signaled me up to the microphone and asked me to make a testimony about my search for my daddy and what it meant to finally find him. I began to tell my story and as I did I felt myself growing. I knew I was becoming complete. Near the end of my testimony, the entire room began to shout, "Praise God" and "Amen." I felt so good basking in God's glory.

  I didn't sleep a wink that night. I called Mama soon as I got back to the hotel and told her I had found daddy and I had went to see him. I don't know why I called Mama first but I just did. Surprisingly she sounded happy for me. She even asked how he was doing. I told her about the strokes and him being sick. Before we got off the phone, she said she would pray for him. Next I called LaWanda. She wasn't as excited as I was but she definitely had a million questions for me. We stayed on the phone for three hours. By the time I called Derick with the news, it was one thirty in the morning. We talked until eight in the morning. When I got off the phone with Derick, I took a shower and went down to the gift shop to buy a camera and some film. There was no way I was going back home without pictures of daddy. I just kept thinking about the last time he had left when we were kids, and all I had in my head all these years was that image of him leaving.

Daddy and Ms. Gail met Ms. Eunice and I at the hotel around one. We went out for lunch and then they drove me to the airport. Ms. Gail made sure she got my home and cell phone numbers and she gave me her cell phone number, too. She said sometimes daddy would be home alone while she ran errands and wouldn't answer the phone. We said our goodbyes at my gate and we all broke down. When I got back to Georgia, Derick and the boys met me at the airport. I was so happy to see them. I told the boys all about how I had finally met their grandfather and they were happy. I think Derick and the boys really understood what that meant to me. We stopped at CVS and dropped the film off to be developed. I could hardly wait during the one hour processing time. I hadn't even unpacked before I was back out the door on my way to CVS to get the pictures. That night Derick, the boys, and me sat around and looked at the pictures. We added them to our family photo album. I slept well that night.

I talked to daddy almost every day since I had been back in Georgia, sometimes several times in a day for several hours. It had been two months since I had found him and I was determined to never lose him again. He told me that he was very sick. I had called a few times and Ms. Gail told me he had to go to the hospital for a few days for treatment. One day I was talking to daddy and I walked past the stand in the living room where we kept some photos and I looked at the photo of me and Derick on our wedding day. Our anniversary was in three weeks and I really wanted to do something special since I had found daddy. I asked daddy would he walk me down the aisle to renew my vows on our anniversary. Without hesitation he said, "yes." I couldn't wait to tell Derick. We started sending out invitations immediately. I wanted all my family and friends to be there. I had special programs made up that gave a short story about my search for daddy and finding him, and finally after all these years he was going to walk me down the aisle.

About four days before the renewal ceremony things started going wrong. First, the company that made the programs hadn't made enough and the person who handled the artwork was

## Finding Daddy

out sick with a cold. Apparently, they discarded the original file once they did the first print. Next, Mama said she didn't know if she would be able to make it because they had been running short at the plant and they needed her. I wanted to pull my hair out. *I needed her!* Then came the worst news of all. Ms. Gail called and said Daddy may not be able to make it if his breathing didn't get better over the next day or two. By this time, daddy was getting really sick and he had to have a portable breathing machine. I felt so down. I called and talked to Ms. Eunice. I could always talk to her when Derick wasn't available. Ms. Eunice said that she would ride down from North Carolina with Ms. Gail and daddy to make sure he got there alright. She said she had worked as a registered nurse for twenty six years. She could help Ms. Gail with daddy. I started crying, I was so happy. Ms. Eunice had been a shining light in my life from the first time I met her. Now all I had to do was hope daddy's breathing improved over the next couple of days.

The day before the anniversary celebration, Ms. Gail and Ms. Eunice called me on three way. At first I thought something had happened to daddy. Then they told me they would be there tomorrow around nine in the morning, they had just booked their rooms. Derick had found someone else to make the programs, now all I was worried about was Mama. Henry and his wife were coming. LaWanda would be there with Darren and my niece and Nana was coming with Ms. Grace. We had invited over a hundred guests and got the best catering service in town with a live band.

The next day at the vow renewal, I kept breaking down and messing up my makeup. Once I knew daddy was there and he was actually going to walk me down the aisle, I couldn't keep it together. I had dreamed about this day since I was a little girl before I had even met Derick and gotten married. The ceremony was beautiful. Daddy actually walked me down the aisle without his portable oxygen tank. He just took hold of my arm and we walked together. It felt magical. Everyone stood up as we walked and they all cheered when I reached Derick's side. When we got to the reception, I introduced Mama to Ms. Gail officially and daddy, Mama, and Ms. Gail talked. Then Ms. Gail left Mama with daddy so they could talk while I introduced her and Ms. Eunice to everyone. Ms. Gail told me that daddy would be turning seventy-one tomorrow. When I announced daddy was going to be turning seventy-one the next day, the entire room started singing happy birthday. All the grand kids gathered around daddy's table and sang along with the room.

I must have made that band play, "Dance with My Father," by Luther Vandross five times. Daddy and I danced and laughed and took pictures. It was a beautiful night. Everyone seemed so happy and I don't think I have ever been happier.

The next day I met Ms. Eunice, Ms. Gail, and daddy at their hotel. We went out for lunch. Daddy started talking to me about his ex-wife Denise and my sister Kim. He said he had to get some things handled back home so that if anything happened to him, his girls would be alright, meaning LaWanda, Kim, and me. He told me that Ms. Gail knew everything there was to know about him and that if there ever came a time he couldn't speak with me for some reason, all I had to do was contact Ms. Gail. I told him that LaWanda and I wanted to come up there for Thanksgiving so we could all spend it together for the first time. Ms. Gail said that it was a great idea and it would be easier on daddy if we traveled to North Carolina. I agreed. We took some more pictures and then they got in the car and I watched them drive away until I couldn't see the car anymore.

# CHAPTER 15
## SHOW DOWN IN ICU

After dad left Georgia, we talked on the phone every day planning our first Thanksgiving together. I could tell dad was weak and was getting sicker. Every time I talked to Ms. Gail she sounded sad. She told me she was scared because the doctors didn't sound like dad was going to recover. He had been rushed to the hospital three times since being back home. Each time I would be up worried sick every night until Ms. Gail called me and told me he would be returning home. Then me and daddy would be right back on the phone talking about how we were going to spend our Thanksgiving. He talked about all the food he wanted us to make and how he was going to eat all he wanted no matter what those doctors said. I was so happy.

Thanksgiving was only a month away. I had been so busy planning Thanksgiving with daddy that I didn't realize my birthday was coming up. A few days before my birthday, I received a letter in the mail from daddy. Puzzled, I looked at the envelope. I didn't understand why daddy would be mailing me a letter when we talked on the phone every day. I tore open the envelope and pulled out a check and a piece of paper that said "HAPPY BIRTHDAY." I looked at the check and saw it was for $1500. I broke down and started crying right there. This was the first time my daddy had actually given me something. We got the support checks when we were younger but that was different. I didn't even want to cash the check. I made a copy of it before I deposited it into my bank account.

A few days before Thanksgiving, I got a call from Ms. Gail while I was at work. Immediately I knew something was wrong.

She told me that daddy had been rushed to the hospital again and this time he had been put in ICU. She said things didn't look good and I should try to get there as soon as I could. I called

LaWanda and told her what happened. I told her I was changing my flight plans from the day after tomorrow to tomorrow morning. I just had to go home and get some things and tell Derick and the boys what was going on.

    I flew out early the next morning and Ms. Gail picked me up from the airport. I could tell by the look on her face daddy was doing badly. We went straight to the hospital and when I walked into the ICU and saw daddy, my legs got weak. He looked so small and he was hooked up to all types of machines. I just started crying and holding his hand. He couldn't talk because of the oxygen machine they had him hooked up to, but he squeezed my hand. We stayed until visiting hours were over. Before we left, we prayed. Then we went back to dad's house. Ms. Gail and I stayed up all night talking about daddy. LaWanda arrived the next day and we all went to the hospital. We spoke with the nurses and they told us that they were going to try and take daddy off the oxygen to see how he did. They said he had developed a bad stomach infection and they didn't know how much they could do to treat it. We all gathered around daddy's bed and prayed after the doctors left. Since they took the oxygen off, dad could talk a little bit but the nurse said he was weak and we shouldn't try and make him talk too much. All dad kept talking about was getting some papers signed before anything happened to him.

    The next day we all spent Thanksgiving at the hospital with daddy. It was so depressing. While we were there, a woman walked in the room and just stood in the doorway staring at us.

    "Can I help you?" LaWanda asked the woman.

    "I'm here to see my father," the girl said, looking past LaWanda over to the bed where I was standing. I looked at her closely and I saw the resemblance to daddy in her features.

    She walked over to the bedside and I saw daddy's face light up like it had when he had first saw me walk in the room. There was no doubt in my mind this was Kim. Daddy introduced us to each other, but I could feel the chill in her attitude. We stayed another hour before leaving Kim alone with daddy. I told Ms. Gail we were going to fly back to Georgia tomorrow. I needed to get some more clothes and check on my family. I promised I would be back Friday.

    When I got back home, I told Derick about daddy's

## Finding Daddy

condition and how our half sister had showed up at the hospital. He offered to fly back out there with me on Friday for moral support. We decided to leave the boys with his parents while we were gone. When we got back out to North Carolina, Ms. Gail met us at the airport but she wasn't driving daddy's car. When I asked her why she wasn't driving daddy's Jaguar she said Kim had come to the house with the police demanding all of daddy's things. Gail said she didn't want to make a scene at the house with his daughter so she just let her take the things. She also said daddy wasn't showing signs of getting better. He had been put back on oxygen and his lung functions were failing. When we got to the hospital, I saw that Kim was in daddy's room with another woman. Ms. Gail said that the woman was Robert's ex-wife. I immediately thought back to the snobbish woman who I had talked to on the phone that time. I was furious. I didn't even speak to them when I came in the room. I wasn't doing this fake thing anymore. I had as much right to this man as they did. But I couldn't stand being around them, so we left after an hour. Derick and I flew back home the next day.

 I spent the next few weeks trying to get my thoughts together and spend a little quality time with my family. My boys missed me. I had been on the move the whole month. I planned to go back to North Carolina to spend Christmas with daddy. I flew out on December 19th. My flight got in kind of late so Ms. Gail and I didn't go to the hospital. We decided we'd go first thing in the morning. When we got to the hospital and buzzed to be let in the ICU, we were informed that they couldn't buzz us through because Mr. Wilson's attorney had left instructions that no one was to be allowed to see him without written consent from the executor of his affairs. We were furious and demanded to see someone. Daddy's doctor came out and spoke with us. He showed us the court order and told us his hands were tied. I read the paperwork and couldn't believe the two signatures at the bottom of the paperwork, Kim and Denise Wilson. We argued that he hadn't been with Denise since the nineties. The doctor was sympathetic but there was nothing he could do. I left the hospital fuming. I called Derick and he stayed on the phone with me all night while I cried.

 We finally caught up with Denise and Kim at the hospital on Christmas day. Kim came out of the ICU and told us that daddy wasn't really up for visitors, but she allowed me to go in for ten minutes. I went in the room and looked at daddy. He looked so bad, I wasn't even sure if he knew I was in the room. I just stood there looking at him. I was sad but I was more upset than anything that daddy had let those two Jezebels trick him into signing those papers. I was also mad that he hadn't taken care of the other paperwork he had talked to me about, before he got in this condition. When I walked back out to the waiting area, I had the urge to just jump on Kim and beat her down, but I held it together until we got outside, then I just lost it. I just cried and cried. When we made it back to the house, I went straight to sleep. I didn't even call Derick and the boys. Before I flew back home, I made a last effort to try and have a relationship with Kim, mainly because I knew I couldn't keep flying back and forth and leaving my family, especially since they had started acting funny with us about coming to see daddy. I left all my information at the hospital for her to call me and keep me updated on daddy's condition. I knew they weren't going to contact Ms. Gail.

## CHAPTER 16
### GONE TO GLORY

I called the hospital every day after I returned to Georgia to speak with the nurses to try and get some information on daddy, but the nurses wouldn't give out on daddy's condition due to the court order Kim and her mother had put in place. I was so frustrated. One of the nurses, I think her name was Beverly, felt sorry for me and told me that daddy had been getting worse since Christmas. I hadn't heard a word from Kim at all. I was furious. How could she do this to us? He was our daddy, too. Outside of Derick, Ms. Gail, and Ms. Eunice, I felt like I was alone in my feelings about what was going on with daddy.

On January 3rd, I got a call from Ms. Gail. She was crying and I knew before she said a word that my daddy was gone. She said daddy had passed away three hours earlier and that Kim and her mother had been at the hospital when he passed. They had called no one. Ms. Gail had just happened to call to see if she could get an update on daddy and they had told her daddy had passed away. I was so hurt. I couldn't believe that my daddy was gone. We had just reconnected six and a half months earlier. I called LaWanda and told her the news. She sounded sad but I really couldn't tell. She agreed to fly out to North Carolina the next day. Next I called Mama and told her. I think Mama was more sad for me than she was at the fact that daddy was gone. Even though they had finally talked at the renewal ceremony, I don't think Mama ever really truly forgave daddy. Derick held me all night while I cried.

The next day LaWanda and I flew to North Carolina. Ms. Gail met us at the airport and we went straight to the hospital. When we got there, the people at the hospital told us the body had been picked up by the funeral home already. They gave us the number of the funeral home and we called. The director of the funeral home confirmed he had the body, but said we couldn't see it at the time because he had to prepare daddy first. The next day when we called the funeral director, he gave us Kim's phone number. When I called her to talk to her about seeing daddy's body, she said that no one could view the body because the military wanted to do their own autopsy since daddy was having a military funeral. She said the autopsy could take weeks. She promised to call us once they made the funeral arrangements. Most of what she had said was a lie, but what could I do? I didn't even know where my daddy's body was.

    I returned back to Georgia more distraught than I had been before I left. A few days later I received a call from a man who said he was daddy's brother. He said his name was Curtis Wilson Jr. I never even knew daddy had a brother. Ms. Gail had given him my number. We talked on the phone for hours that night and he told me so many things about my daddy. He told me how daddy used to talk about LaWanda and I and how his face would light up whenever he talked about his girls. He also told me I had two aunts who lived in Philadelphia. Talking to Uncle Curtis made me feel ten times better. He made me feel like I still had a connection to daddy. Eventually, it was Uncle Curtis who let me know about the funeral arrangements. Kim and Denise were still playing games. They kept changing the funeral home and the burial date. They did it so many times, Daddy's sisters stopped contacting them and ultimately missed the funeral altogether.

    My Uncle Curtis called the day before the funeral and told me they were having the funeral the next day. He said he had just gotten to North Carolina. He said Kim and Denise had held the wake last night and he didn't know until the last minute. He said Ms. Gail had attended the wake. The next thing he said broke my heart. He told me that Kim and Denise had daddy cremated about two hours ago. When he told me this, I almost fainted and luckily Derick came running when he heard me scream and caught me in his arms. I called Ms. Eunice and told her what happened and she started crying. She said she had attended the wake the night before and said if she knew they were going to cremate the body she would've taken a picture for me.

    Derick and I flew out that night. The next day we met up with my Uncle Curtis early in the morning at his hotel. He looked

## Finding Daddy

so much like daddy, I just broke down. We were waiting for Kim to call Uncle Curtis with directions to the church. We were all upset about them cremating the body. Kim had told Uncle Curtis they had to cremate the body because it had been sitting too long by the time the military finished their autopsy. None of us believed it. The final straw was when Kim didn't call but sent a car to pick us up. We sent the car back after the driver told us where the funeral was being held. When we got to the church, it didn't even seem like we were there to pay respects to my father. It looked more like a stand off. Denise and Kim stood on one side of the church with their family and we stood on the other. I know the soldiers that were attending were confused. At the cemetery there was no real burial since daddy had been cremated. The army just had some soldiers give daddy the twenty-one gun salute, folded the flag, and gave it to Denise. And just like that it was over.

When I got back to Georgia, I began to look into daddy's will. Ms. Gail had claimed daddy had gotten a legal separation from Denise years ago, but she couldn't find the paperwork. She suspected Kim had taken the papers when she came by to get daddy's things that time. She claimed Kim and Denise had forged some papers to try and take control of daddy's assets. She said she had filed paperwork in the courthouse to put a freeze on all of daddy's estate. I refused to let them do this. I told Ms. Gail I was going to hire an attorney and we were going to fight this. To date, I am still in a pending legal battle over my daddy's estate with my sister Kim and her mother Denise. I had prepared myself for daddy's death, but I wasn't prepared for all the antics I had to endure from Kim and Denise. I found my daddy. Now it seems like I am starting a new search for proper closure.

***THE END.***

# *ABOUT THE AUTHOR*

Renita Gibbs is a passionate, powerful, phenomenal woman of God, called upon to uplift individuals with the tools of knowledge she procured while laboring in Corporate America. Renita was born in Augusta, GA and is the youngest of three children. She received her B.S degree in Criminal Law from Voorhees College in Denmark, South Carolina. Ms. Gibbs is married to Derick Gibbs Sr. They have celebrated 14 years of a healthy, fruitful and vibrant relationship. They were blessed with two wonderful sons, Derick Jr. and Daniel. She resides in Atlanta, GA and currently serves as President of Gibbs Empowerment, L.L.C, an organization which empowers individuals to live up to their fullest potential.

Ms. Gibbs is no stranger to network and marketing. She has been in the business for over 17 years. Ms. Gibbs is using her network and marketing skills as her vehicle to financial freedom. She stands on integrity and puts God first in everything she does. Ms. Gibbs is currently available to speak at any function that is geared toward wealth, success, healthy living and personal development. Ms. Gibbs' motto is 'When you know better, you do better!'

Please feel free to contact Renita to find out about her workshops, personal appearances, and keynote presentations. She may be contacted at:

Gibbs Empowerment L.L.C
P.O Box 743154
Riverdale, GA 30274
Phone: 678.820.8870
Email: info@renitagibbs.com
Website: www.renitagibbs.com

To order copies for $14.95, go to
www.amazon.com or
www.createspace/3537181

Made in the USA
Charleston, SC
17 March 2014